The History of England

An Introduction to Centuries of English Culture, Kings & Queens, Key Events, Battles and More

HISTORY BROUGHT ALIVE

© Copyright 2022 - All rights reserved.

The content contained within this book may not be reproduced, duplicated, or transmitted without direct written permission from the author or the publisher.

Under no circumstances will any blame or legal responsibility be held against the publisher, or author, for any damages, reparation, or monetary loss due to the information contained within this book, either directly or indirectly.

Legal Notice:

This book is copyright protected. It is only for personal use. You cannot amend, distribute, sell, use, quote, or paraphrase any part, or the content within this book, without the consent of the author or publisher.

Disclaimer Notice:

Please note the information contained within this document is for educational and entertainment purposes only. All effort has been executed to present accurate, up-to-date, reliable, complete information. No warranties of any kind are declared or implied. Readers acknowledge that the author is not engaged in the rendering of legal, financial, medical, or professional advice. The content within this book has been derived from various sources. Please consult a licensed professional before attempting any techniques outlined in this book.

By reading this document, the reader agrees that under no circumstances is the author responsible for any losses, direct or indirect, that are incurred as a result of the use of the information contained within this document, including, but not limited to, errors, omissions, or inaccuracies.

FREE BONUS FROM HBA: EBOOK BUNDLE

Greetings!

First of all, thank you for reading our books. As fellow passionate readers of History and Mythology, we aim to create the very best books for our readers.

Now, we invite you to join our VIP list. As a welcome gift, we offer the History & Mythology Ebook Bundle below for free. Plus you can be the first to receive new books and exclusives! Remember it's 100% free to join.

Simply scan the QR code to join.

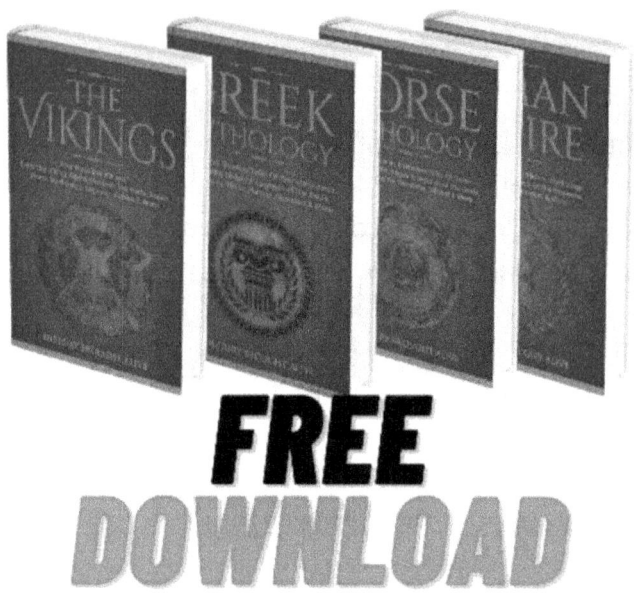

Keep up to date with us on:
YouTube: History Brought Alive
Facebook: History Brought Alive
www.historybroughtalive.com

CONTENTS

INTRODUCTION 1

CHAPTER 1: STORIES ABOUT ENGLAND 7

MYTHS AND LEGENDS 8
RELIGIONS 13
FAST FACTS 15
TRUTH VS MEDIA PORTRAYALS 16

CHAPTER 2: THE TIMELINE BEGINS, 410-1066 AD, THE ANGLO-SAXONS PERIOD 18

ANGLO-SAXONS 20
THE NORMAN CONQUEST 22

CHAPTER 3: 1066-1450 AD, ENGLAND'S MEDIEVAL AND MIDDLE AGES 25

MAGNA CARTA 26
THE BLACK DEATH 29
THE PEASANTS' REVOLT 31
THE HUNDRED YEARS' WAR: 1337–1453 33

CHAPTER 4: THE HOUSE OF TUDOR AND BEYOND 36

THE WAR OF THE ROSES 37
THE TUDORS 41
THE RENAISSANCE 47

CHAPTER 5: ENGLAND AND THE "AGE OF MODERNITY" 51

ENGLISH CIVIL WARS 52
THE GLORIOUS REVOLUTION: 1688–1689 56
AGE OF ENLIGHTENMENT 58

CHAPTER 6: GEORGIAN ENGLAND 61

    Jacobite Rebellion 62
    Acts of Union 65
    Political Parties 67
    The American Revolution 69

CHAPTER 7: VICTORIAN ENGLAND 74

    The English Government in Victorian Times 76
    Imperial Era 78
    Industrial Revolution 80
    Intellectual Accomplishments 82

CHAPTER 8: THE WORLD AT WAR 88

    The First World War: 1914–1918 91
    The Interwar Years: 1918–1939 101
    The Second World War: 1939–1945 106

CHAPTER 9: MODERN ENGLAND 125

    The Decline of the British Empire 126
    The Welfare State: 1945–1979 128
    Thatcherism: 1979–1990 130
    Brexit 132

CONCLUSION 137

APPENDIX: KINGS, QUEENS, AND PRIME MINISTERS OF ENGLAND 141

REFERENCES 149

INTRODUCTION

The history of any country is complex. However, that of England is perhaps one of the most complex and varied histories of any country. This is not to say that England's history is especially more misunderstood, misrepresented, or intricate. Nor is it to imply that the history of other countries, Western or otherwise, is of inferior interest or development when compared to England's. But when a country has a history with such substantial longevity as England's, it is bound to be intimidating to those hoping for a succinct summary.

Many historians, educators, and general authors alike have attempted to tackle England's history. There have been countless textbooks, guidebooks, and tomes that attempt to give a clear and concise image of England's chronology. Many of them follow the same chronological structure that will be adhered to in this book, but the difference among many of those books is the pacing, tone, and energy. To put it bluntly, it is easy to write a dense book on England's history. If they do not follow a clear chronological timeline, then they can be difficult to follow. The sheer amount of events, characters, and settings within England's history makes it nearly impossible to structure a book in any other way than according to time. To create themes or sections devoted to any other categorization is to confuse the reader, giving a false understanding of the series of events and the cultural and social factors that contributed to the development of England's history as a whole. But, books following the chronological structure are not exempt from fault either. Some adhere to a strong academic and/or scholarly tone. They expect readers to be experts in the field they are entering, omitting opportunities to give a clear background on events and changes throughout history. This is understandable, considering that to give a comprehensive history of England is to demand a substantial effort from the reader. Unfortunately, many historians and scholars see this as a challenge worth facing, writing books that only fellow scholars can understand. This makes it difficult for the common person to approach the topic of England's history outside of an Advanced Placement history class.

In an effort to even dip one's toe into the history of England, the amateur scholar is thrown back, ostracized by the overcomplicated and dull quality of rigorous history books. To be clear, there is a time and a place for these books. Scholars and historians, and students of these areas, are likely to gravitate toward specialized books. They are the demographic that these books are geared toward and written for. But, for the common person, who Shakespeare can attest is arguably the most important member of the population, this level of complexity is unnecessary. You do not begin to study history as an expert.

The book you hold in your hands attempts to combat this. *The History of England* is neither comprehensive nor of the same caliber as highbrow academic or rigorous scholarly texts. It does not attempt to be either of these, though, as you will discover throughout the narrative. Its goal is, instead, to show the reader a different side of the study of history. History, as a general area of interest, does not need to be dull or heavy material. In fact, it should be as fascinating and thrilling as history itself. We do not read stories to prove to others our literary endurance nor to flex our vocabulary. We read stories to be entertained, to discover ourselves within them. We read about the past to better understand our own present.

In *The History of England*, the reader will encounter poignant and verifiably factual information. It will cover a broad overview of England's most pertinent historical events and figures. It will detail key cultural, social, and economic changes. Compared to other history books addressing England's history, it is a refreshing read that is both easily comprehensible and factually correct. The book will give a more concise history, told in chronological order and supplemented with an additional list of the English monarchy and heads of Parliament in order to help guide further research.

History Brought Alive is made up of a team of experts in history and mythology. Their writers have established credibility in their fields and aim to create a pleasant, genuine, and educational reading experience for anyone interested in broadening their historical studies. History Brought Alive's writers take pride in their work and strive to make academic and scholarly material accessible to anyone. They have a wide variety of writers, each with expertise in different geographical histories, spanning from Norse mythology to Roman history to Hoodoo, the history of ancient spiritual connections. Their books are well-referenced and accurate, supporting the History Brought Alive name and creating a foundation of meaningful historical texts.

The writers at History Brought Alive understand the importance of creating a beneficial historical text. As a result, *The History of England* presents highlights of the key events in England's history. It aims not to confuse or intimidate but to entice and engage, creating a satisfying read of a true account. It gives readers a taste of the country's rich history in a variety of different areas.

The History of England is a masterful book for anyone wanting to learn more about English history and culture. It takes the reader through a panorama of historical events, giving the reader an emotional and human experience. It doesn't drown the reader in statistics but appeals, instead, to the origin of storytelling. It is a narrative, first and foremost, to be enjoyed and to elicit passion from the reader. For anyone, whether you are a scholar, a student, a casual reader, or someone who simply hopes to have an intelligent conversational topic for next year's Thanksgiving dinner, this is a must-have for your library.

Reading other books on England's history, especially as an introduction to the topic, is time-consuming and could result in the reader simply disliking a topic out of misunderstanding. In order to best understand the true, fascinating nature of England's history, *The History of England* is the text at the top of your list. History is not meant to be sitting on a dusty shelf or at the bottom of your reading pile. It is not meant to remain inside the classroom. It is not a subject for the elite, for a specialized few who choose to remain within the confines of the university system. History is for everyone. History is intended to be brought alive and to live alongside us.

CHAPTER 1

Stories About England

England is already a land of stories, as long as we are only willing to recognize which ones are truthful and which ones are simply reflections of our own contemporary beliefs about the country. Considering how long England has been around and how much of an impact it has had on the world, it comes as no surprise that stories about the country are infinite and span from incredible cultural and social commentary that has left a meaningful stamp on the nation, to incorrect stereotypes. It has been the center of folklore, television shows, myths, and movies. Both the stories that have originated in England and those that seek to portray it from an outsider's perspective have had lasting impacts on our impressions of the English people as well as English history and culture.

In this section, you will be given a brief overview of how both scholars and common people consider modern England today. Like any other nation, England has been affected (both internally and externally) by the stories told about it and the stories that have been told within its borders. A story makes a story, in truth, and England's history and present time would not be the same without the stories that came out of its nation. Some of the most influential myths and legends of England's history have shaped the moral conduct and beliefs of its people. Similarly, the media concerning England today still impacts how the British people think of themselves and how others think of them. While the history of a place must be understood to see the place for what it is now, it is equally important to first assess where you, as the reader, stand now: Evaluate the language you use and the knowledge that you currently have. It is important to begin with what you know and to ask yourself how you know it. A beginning is always the start before one dives into the past.

Myths and Legends

The myths and legends that have perpetuated English history and culture are similar to other countries' myths and legends in that they act as mirrors for what their people value as well as reinforce the forward progression of the country's future. One of England's most popular and enduring myths is that of Robin Hood. Though some may only recognize him as Kevin Costner and others might identify with the Disney production featuring foxes, a lion king who sucks his thumb, and a bear with a rather striking resemblance to Baloo from a sister Disney film, the true legend appears in history around the 12th century, during King John of England's reign. While the man himself is still unidentified, there are several theories as to who such a humanitarian and vigilante might have been. The time and origin of the myth suggest, though, that the factuality of such a myth is irrelevant when it comes to the importance that it bore on popular culture and English culture.

If you're unfamiliar with the myth of Robin Hood, it goes as follows: A young man during the 12th century robs from the rich to feed the poor, gaining help from his band of Merry Men and his faithful friend Little John. Now, given the time period in which this myth arises, it is no surprise that such a legend became necessary. The origin of any myth or legend is in necessity, a desperation of the people to believe in something. This can be seen in contemporary myths as well. Superheroes are created for the same purpose: They provide beacons of hope for both the young and old in times that challenge the hearts and souls of the common people. During King John of England's reign, the people of England were indeed heavily taxed; this much is true from the original Robin Hood myth. King John's reign ended with the signing of the Magna Carta, a momentous event that will be detailed later in Chapter Three, and the subsequent cessation of the feudal system in England. Citizens of the country were growing tired of a system that relied on their hard work and left them with nothing to their name, all for the greater good of the monarchy overseeing their homelands. A vigilante, romanticized or not, who restored some of the power to the common people was necessitated at the time and, therefore, became incredibly popular. It would prove to have lasting effects on the people and the modern impression of England.

One theory of the true Robin Hood is that it was really a man named Robert Godberd, who did in fact travel around Nottinghamshire to rob the rich. However, his "robbing the rich to feed the poor" narrative has been gentrified to meet a modern audience. His true actions, according to historians, would have more likely been murder, arson, burgling, and harassment of travelers and clergy. Where the contemporary myth draws more inspiration from true history is in King John's passing of the Forest Law, which gave private access to forested hunting grounds to the monarchy as well as the feudal lords. Unsurprisingly, it was unpopular among the public, and Godberd's actions against the clergy and feudal lords seemed heroic at the time, as he and his band of "merry men" fought back against the iron grip of their government.

The debates among historians regarding the myth of King Arthur are similar to that of Robin Hood. The chances that such a legend existed are probable, considering the circumstances of the time in which King Arthur was supposed to have lived, though historians have yet to confirm whether this is true. With a history as long as England's, it is difficult to differentiate the truth from a perpetuated myth that has become so ingrained in the culture that it seems plausible.

The myth of King Arthur first appears in Welsh poetry around the 10th century, claiming that King Arthur won 12 battles against too many different enemies to make such a story possible. Furthermore, the stories detailed in the poems document that the battles took place in disparate locations, making it impossible for a single person to have been at all 12. That being said, the myth of a King Arthur stuck and continued to spread throughout English history. King Arthur earns his first full life story in the 12th-century book *The History of the Kings of Britain*, in which Lancelot, Guinevere, and Excalibur make their first appearances. The story was a perfect combination of myth and truth, pulled from other stories of real kings and heroes of the time, creating an invaluable narrative for English culture.

The power of the King Arthur myth was lasting in English culture, in that as it developed, it evolved from a single tale of a powerful king to a tale of a young stable hand rising to power. In essence, it is one of the oldest rags-to-riches stories to have entered the modern canon. Its mythic power grew extensively as time went on, becoming a common tale for everyone to point to for inspiration and heroism. Kings and queens, as well as artists, poets, and the common citizens of England, would herald the myth of King Arthur as truth for centuries to come.

Though the story of Jack and the Beanstalk might not carry as much weight as the former English stories, its importance in English culture cannot be understated. The story was documented in its first written form in 1734 under the name "The Story of Jack Spriggins and the Enchanted Bean." Prior to this, though, it is perhaps one of the oldest oral stories of English culture. Some historians believe that it predates most classical mythology and was first told more than 5,000 years ago, when Western and Eastern Indo-European languages split. Even though Jack and the Beanstalk is not a story that carries as much heroism or social commentary, it offers a different sort of importance for English culture in that it targets English children specifically. By offering moral lessons, some that predate England itself, it implores that English children grow up with a foundation of honesty, trustworthiness, and humility. Though children's tales may not garner as much attention as those that adults tend to favor, it is the children's tales that, arguably, create the most impact.

Religions

England's connection to religion today is most obviously represented by the monarchy. In modern news and tabloids, the traditions and customs of the monarchy are often coupled with the traditions of the Catholic Church. And while this isn't incorrect, in that the monarchy itself is a traditionally Catholic institution, the representations of the English monarchy are not the sole encompassing of religious customs in

England.

England has remained predominantly Christian from its inception, though the denominations have changed slightly. While in its origins England was mostly Roman Catholic and Anglican (after the establishment of the Church of England in the sixth century), now there are more members of the Methodist denomination as well as Islam in England.

According to a 2001 study, almost five million people have been baptized in the Catholic Church, making it the second largest religious following still in England. It falls second only to the Church of England, which has 26 million people within its following ("How many Catholics," 2010). Now, considering the date of these statistics, it's probably a safe assumption that they have increased, but with religion becoming increasingly unpopular and more of a private aspect of people's lives rather than a public following, there are fewer published reports to consult.

Currently, Islam is the fastest growing religion in England, with Judaism behind it, though they are paltry percentages compared to those of the Christian following in the country. As a whole, England is a relatively religious country. It remains tied to its roots, and while it currently advertises the freedom of religion for its citizens, the connections that it still holds to the past are evident in daily life.

Fast Facts

Before diving into the past, having a firm idea of contemporary England may be helpful. England boasts a proud age of over 800,000 years. It has survived countless wars, a long line of colonial control, and successful relationships with powerful nations that still exist today, bolstering the country and providing vital support for other countries around the world. Its government is a combination of the British monarchy and a parliamentary system. It is ruled by both a monarch (either a king or a queen) and a prime minister. While today the monarchy functions as more of a figurehead for the country, its citizens carry a strong sense of pride for their king or queen, as is evident by their withstanding presence in media and culture. The prime minister, on the other hand, now does most of the governmental functions that dictate the direction of the country itself. As a modern country, it is a proud country, one that has a lengthy history and a population of 55 million, as of 2016 ("Population of England 2016," n.d.). It was the first industrialized nation in the world (a story that will be detailed further in the coming chapters) and is still considered one of the world's leading powers.

Truth vs Media Portrayals

Despite being a world power in both history and the contemporary world, England has a problematic relationship with its media portrayals. It has made appearances in many different films and television shows, many of which are period dramas. While this is entertaining to viewers, it paints an unrealistic picture of England as a country. For instance, the television show *Downton Abbey* was immensely popular on an international scale. It followed an upper-class family in the early 18th century, documenting their trials as well as the stories of their servants. It was a portrayal of how the English upper echelon changed as England entered the modern era. It was inarguably a media sensation; however, when television shows like *Downton Abbey* or *Call the Midwife* are coupled with countless period films (most of which take place during the Elizabethan era), it shows that England has stagnated in a culture of the past. If all that is shown of England in the media is of England's history, then it's only natural for viewers to assume that there is nothing of contemporary interest in England today. Their culture is no more, in essence. Viewers might also assume that social customs and cultural expectations are aligned with antiquated ideals when of course this is not the case.

The reader is encouraged to understand that as they learn about England's past, it does not negate where England is today. It is not a representation of contemporary England, but rather an explanation of how it came to be what it is now.

CHAPTER 2

The Timeline Begins, 410-1066 Ad, the Anglo-Saxons Period

The Anglo-Saxon period in England began in the 5th century when the first settlers came to the land that would become the United Kingdom. The first settlers to arrive in the land were actually invited by the King himself, as defenders of the area from nearby Scots and Picts. Those who came to defend the land were from three tribes—the Angles, the Saxons, and the Jutes—thus giving way to the name of the era in which England was entering. The tribes that came to England would help to define the next few centuries, laying the foundation of the country that would become one of the most powerful and influential in the world. Despite England being founded upon a group of people brought together from different tribes, it would find several unifying forces to create a stable and formative country on its journey to become "the nation of the English." Though the tribes succeeded in defending the territory from the Scots and Picts, it wasn't exempt from further division among its people. The England of the fifth century was a collection of kingdoms that did not recognize a single ruler until the ninth century when the southern regions acknowledged a single lordship as responsible for them. But recognizing lordships and accepting temporary communions was just the start of England becoming a cohesive kingdom.

Religion, Christianity specifically, was introduced to England as a way to unify the nation. By the end of the 5th century, England was still divided into separate countries, but they had all recognized Christianity as a single ruling ideology that governed their systems. It should be recognized that at this time in history, there was no chance of a separation between church and state. In fact, this far back in history, the Church acted in place of a single governing state and helped to initiate the laws and social and cultural rules that would eventually be taken up by the state (or the centralized governments). It was from here that England officially entered what is known as the Anglo-Saxon period, during which the Church and the group of settlers first to arrive in England laid the groundwork for the country to come.

Anglo-Saxons

With the fall of the Roman empire in the early fifth century, a power vacuum surged and competing tribes began fighting over the territory of England. After many battles, the tribes that became collectively known as the Anglo-Saxons won out, obtaining power over England. As the Anglo-Saxons, or the governing unit of the English kingdoms, took power, they began to institute customs and rules for the new kingdoms that would come together to form England. Furthermore, the Anglo-Saxon period, previously known as the Dark Ages, in England's history was tumultuous and riddled with invasions. Nations were new and unstable, but the recent group of settlers was determined to create a new kingdom for themselves. The Anglo-Saxons established early farms, trading concepts, and a language. They spoke what we now term "Old English" and brought literacy to the area. While the knowledge pertaining to them is limited, considering the time frame of their existence, their presence was pertinent to the development of England. Their occupation in England marks the transformative period between Roman rule and the Norman conquest, denoting the end of the Anglo-Saxon period.

It was during the time of the Anglo-Saxons that England was at its most perilous concerning invasions from Vikings. While there are many competing narratives about the Vikings, simply put, they were the second group of settlers that migrated to the area now known as England alongside the Anglo-Saxons. Much like the Anglo-Saxons, the Vikings were made up of three nations of people who, over time and colloquialisms, became merged into two groups of Vikings. Originally, Vikings were classified as either Danish or Swedish Vikings. Not much is known about Swedish Vikings, but it is worthy of note that they were part of the groups that helped to conquer parts of England, even if they were a group that fell to the wayside over time. Eventually, the Danish Vikings, or the Danes, would become what is now commonly referred to as, simply, the Vikings.

Compared to the Anglo-Saxons, the Vikings were considered barbaric pirates, a seafaring population that concerned itself more with warfare than developing settlements. When both tribes claimed territories of England from the Romans, the Vikings and the Anglo-Saxons became neighbors. The main difference between the two neighbor tribes was that of culture. The Anglo-Saxons were overwhelmingly more literate than the Vikings and brought with them the foundations for the English language, much of which is still used today in England. The

Anglo-Saxons were also practitioners of the Anglo-Saxon Church, which was the Roman Catholic Church at the time. With their devout following, they practiced "morally righteous" behaviors, compared to those of Vikings. Since warfare was less of a priority in comparison to piety, the Anglo-Saxons could also devote more time and resources to infrastructure. As a result, they built many of the first churches in England, some of which are still standing today, including Westminster Abbey. Ultimately, as time went on, the Anglo-Saxons won over the Viking territory, pushing their neighbor tribe into near obsoletion.

The Norman Conquest

The Norman conquest marks the end of the Anglo-Saxon period. At the start of the 11th century, the previous King Edward had chosen a son of a nobleman, Harold Godwinson, to be the next king of England. William, the Duke of nearby Normandy, decided to launch an invasion of England. What began as a personal slight against the Duke, who had been promised the title King of England, soon became the most influential invasion in England's history, changing England's social, cultural, and economic spheres forever. Alongside William's endeavors to take the throne were other challengers to the English crown. It was a new nation, but many leaders recognized it as a valuable asset. Both Harald III of Norway and his brother, Tostig, launched attacks to obtain the title of the King of England. Though William, the Duke of Normandy, wasn't directly impacted by these other challengers, the additional conflict helped to destabilize King Harold Godwinson, allowing him to win the conflict.

In 1066, at the famous Battle of Hastings, William successfully conquered England, marking it the last successful conquest of England. His lineage would officially begin the monarchy that would remain through current times. Throughout his rule, King William survived many attacks on his crown, but he held his kingdom fast and maintained rule over England. Though King William would contribute much to the country of England, on a moral note, he would establish a reputation for victory. England would face many enemies over the long span of its history, but by the strength of itself as a nation, it would continue to prevail.

The long-term effects of the Norman conquest would be tenfold for England. As both a king and a military general, King William instituted new military strategies in England. He built castles within his territory as battle defense stations. These castles would remain standing and in use for hundreds of years. It was also under King William that construction for the Tower of London and Oxford University began. On a cultural level, the Norman conquest was immensely propulsive for English culture. Since King William was from Normandy, and not from England, he brought with him a new social structure. He introduced Norman landowners to England, replacing the English landowning elite and laying the groundwork for feudalism, the economic and social system that would remain in England for the next 600 years. Citizens could now own land in exchange for military service, changing how people obtained land and how they thought about military service. The hallowed Anglo-Saxon Church changed as well under King William's rule after he brought Norman clergy into the Church. On an international level, King William's conquest brought England closer to France. His ruling introduced the French language to England, marrying some of their vocabularies, and connected England to France with economic and political ties. These ties would remain for the duration of England's existence and is still a relationship maintained today.

CHAPTER 3

1066-1450 ad, England's Medieval and Middle Ages

The Late or High Middle Ages began after William the Conqueror's formative reign in England, spanning from approximately 1100–1450 AD. If the Anglo-Saxon period was tumultuous in the sense that every country's beginning is tumultuous, then the Middle Ages were tumultuous in the same sense of a country's childhood. There were a thousand questions to be answered, and England was still discovering itself as a country. Socially speaking, this is the period in which it is perhaps easiest to imagine England. It was a structure of serfdom and monarchy, with feudalism (the system of hierarchy with lords controlling the lands of the public, obtaining labor, funds, and goods from those who lived on it) in full force. After Henry I died in 1135, King William's grandson, Stephen, took the throne and led England into a civil war that would last for the next twenty years. When Henry II took control of England after Stephen, England found a temporary period of peace, until King John (the acclaimed King John of the Robin Hood tales) assumed power and plunged the country into strife once more. He was a ruthless king, with little moral compass. At this time, the Church acted parallel to the monarchy, helping to enact decrees while simultaneously attempting to offer the common people some sort of hope and salvation. The monarchy was the sole governance of England, leaving little room for interpretation or independence. There was no such thing as representation, and the king's orders were the only orders (with the exception of religious standards) that controlled people's lives. If England was going to continue to evolve as a modern country, things would need to change.

Magna Carta

Finally, with the succession of Henry III, England took a turn for social and political advancement with the establishment of Parliament in the momentous passing of the Magna Carta. The public had grown tired of kings ruling as tyrants, and the country was on the verge of rebellion after facing years of abuse under King John's rule. Though it was technically during King Henry III's rule when the Magna Carta took effect, it was not King Henry III himself who signed it. When his father, King John, died when Henry was just nine years old, the young king had no concept of the turmoil he was inheriting. The Magna Carta saw its first drafts in 1215 and 1216, during King John's last years alive as ruler. He served as a tumultuous king, one of the only to be excommunicated and deeply hated by his subjects. It was a pope under his rule that suggested the Magna Carta take effect. If King John signed it into ruling, then the document would restrict all sovereign leaders to a series of laws, designed to limit the oppression of subjects. It was, unsurprisingly, very unpopular with King John, and it took his death for the document to become successful. After King John died and Henry III took the throne, his advisors pushed him to reissue it. The young king took out some of the most controversial amendments that his father had required to be added in order to gain favor as a new king. The Magna Carta went through another round of revision in 1225, but all versions after that would herald back to the 1225 revision as the "final copy."

The Magna Carta was a groundbreaking

document, not just for England but for all other emerging countries. Never before had rulers been held accountable, tyranny abounding and oppression forming the backbone of progress. Furthermore, England was taking a step toward recognizing its people as individuals. This idea would not fully be grasped or utilized until the English Renaissance and then again in the Modern eras, in which individualism would birth social reform. With England passing the Magna Carta, they were taking the first step toward a more evolved and civilized empire. England would continue to take such steps throughout its history, often being the first to revolutionize political ideas. It would repeat this again with the Paris Treaty, the Acts of Union, and the United Nations. England would soon be known as the brainchild of many of the most important governmental documents that the world still knows today. Perhaps it can be attributed to the emphasis placed on intellect, or perhaps it is simply a reflection of the country's ability to adapt with the times. Either way, England would continue to propel politics and government bodies forward toward the future. Five hundred years later, with a burgeoning new rebellion on the other side of the Atlantic Ocean, the colonies that would become the United States of America would point to this very document as evidence of one's right to personal freedom from a sovereign leader.

The Black Death

While King Henry III's rule was predominantly one of peace, ushering in new laws to protect the people against their sovereign leaders and implementing Parliament to further institute representation in the law-making process, it was a short-lived period before English citizens found themselves in yet another period of strife. The Black Death, or the Plague, was the most deadly virus to sweep the nation of England in its entire history. It was a bubonic plague that spread across Europe and Asia from 1346–1353, though it also included several surges in later years. While it is difficult to estimate exactly the toll that the Black Death took on England, due to inaccurate records of the time, it's believed that over 200 million people died throughout Europe, 1.5 million of them hailing from England. The virus is said to have originated in Asia, a parasite carried by rats brought to England. With poor living standards and any sort of personal-hygiene rules nonexistent, the virus turned into a pandemic that raged throughout England. The Black Death, though devastating to the English people, also played a vital role in shaping the world. It would act as a sort of reset for the population, forcing people to re-evaluate labor, living situations, economics, art, and social structures. With such a drastically reduced population, England would be required to reassess everything they thought they had decided upon in the past thousand years.

Economically speaking, the Black Death took an immense toll on England. With the major port cities along the Mediterranean hit the hardest due to the highest populations, trade suffered for England. As a result, trade and economic prosperity all but stagnated during the worst years of the Black Death. The Black Death also affected political spheres, though this is perhaps more oblique than the economic and social effects. Since the plague affected the young, old, poor, and rich, all populations were impacted detrimentally. The monarchs who did survive the Black Death were strained at this time, as is the case for any political structure during times of strife. People looked for answers, for assistance as their lives and the people that they loved fell apart around them. They looked to their government for that help, but with little knowledge about the Black Death, monarchs were at a loss for what to do to support their kingdoms.

The Peasants' Revolt

The reasons for the Peasants' Revolt of 1381 are many, as most disagreements in history tend to be. After the Black Death killed half of the population in England, the remaining workers discovered that they could demand higher wages for their labor. Employers had a smaller population to pull from, leaving them with fewer choices when it came to giving in to workers' stipulations. This lasted for a while, but eventually employers had enough and turned to the government for some sort of regulation to be passed to return the peasants' to their place. In 1351, Parliament passed the Statute of Laborers, which lowered wages to the levels before the Black Death wiped out half of the working population. This angered the workers, who felt they deserved more substantial compensation for their labor. John Ball, a radical preacher who had been excommunicated by the Church and traveled England urging peasants to break from the feudal system, was a second catalyst for the Peasants' Revolt. His preachings inspired citizens to rebel, giving them another incentive to strike back. In 1377, two final events pushed the peasants of England toward revolt. With England at war with France, Parliament passed a new poll tax on English citizens to pay for the war. This set the common people back financially, placing yet another stressor on their lives. Finally, in the same year, King Edward III died, leaving his ten-year-old son, King Richard II, in power. Peasants decided to seize the moment to pressure a new king to make changes that might benefit their lives.

Led by a man named Wat Tyler, peasants marched on London in May 1381. English citizens were joined by others from Norfolk and Suffolk, burning buildings and freeing prisoners as signs to the sovereignty that they had had enough and would no longer play as pawns in their chess game. Eventually, they convinced King Richard to meet with them, demanding that he abolish serfdom. Though young, King Richard was not fooled by the revolt and promised to abolish serfdom as their new king. The peasants relinquished their challenge to the king and returned to their lives. While King Richard did not actually abolish serfdom, the Peasants' Revolt of 1381 would prove to be a vital example of England's lower class taking a stand for themselves against the sovereignty. England's resilience and persistence against oppression would not dim as the country continued to develop.

The Hundred Years' War: 1337–1453

History does not occur in a vacuum. While historians and scholars discuss events individually so that students have a chance to best understand the complexity of each occurrence in history, they do not happen in isolation. Events overlap, many occurring simultaneously. It's important to remember this as one progresses through the timeline of England's history and each event is detailed. They are not happening independently but rather impacting one another simultaneously. While the Black Death was raging across Europe and Asia, the Hundred Years' War had already begun between England and France. Due to the early ties of William the Conqueror, England and France had already been tethered as trade and political partners.

The Hundred Years' War that occurred during the late Middle Ages had many driving factors, including years of prior tension between England and France's monarchies. In the immediate years leading up to it, the main events that drove England and France to conflict were those concerning the French crown and the territory known as the duchy of Guyenne. The territory was technically owned by England but had long been recognized as belonging to the French crown. As England grew as a kingdom, they wanted the territory back from France's claim. Secondly, in 1328, France's Charles IV died, with the last known living relatives living in the English monarchy, giving the English reason to claim the French crown.

France was unwilling to acquiesce to England, ensuing a hundred years' worth of conflict. Now, considering the length of the war, the Hundred Years' War was not as constant as other wars in history. It was more a series of battles that paused and began again over a span of a hundred years. The war went on several hiatuses, being picked up by several English kings as the years progressed. What occurred during the Hundred Years' War was an advancement of military developments and a sign of England's power.

When Henry V renewed the war in 1415, the English proved victorious with their superior military techniques and equipment at the famous battle of Normandy. He tried to claim political power in France at the time, too, crowning himself the king of France as well as the king of England. France would have no way with him, though, and surged against him, Joan of Arc leading the way in the siege of Orleans.

The French army regathered and reorganized itself, coming back with fresh forces and military tactics. They reclaimed both Burgundy and the duchy of Guyenne, proving military prowess. Though the war never ended formally in a treaty, the English accepted that the French had grown their military and political powers to protect their own kingdom and no longer laid siege to them.

The time would come again when England and France would go to war with one another, becoming a common thread along English history and making the Hundred Years' War only the spark in a fire of conflicts between the two countries.

CHAPTER 4

The House of Tudor and Beyond

The Tudor dynasty has become the object of many historians' interest and media representations alike. The popular television show *Tudors* capitalized upon the reputation of Henry VIII and his sensational lineage. Entertainment has turned the House of Tudor into a romanticized and embellished family of shockingly lewd behaviors, but the Tudors were a lasting dynasty for a reason. They did not endure simply because their behaviors were questionable according to the Church. They were methodical and made great social and political changes that had a lasting impact on England.

Under the famous Tudor dynasty, England would most notably undergo religious changes that would both upset the public and the Church. Though it resulted in many conflicts on the civilian level, it would also spark a new idea in England's public and political leaders. The idea of the separation of church and state would be planted during this time. With the tumultuous changes, the separation would seem inevitable and almost an easier option than keeping the two tethered. Of course, the true separation would not actually occur until much later in England's history, but with the leaders of the Tudor dynasty making drastic and modern changes to the religion of the country, it showed people that religion was not as rigid as they might have once believed but, in fact, a flexible and adaptable part of life. This would prove challenging with the Church, but would also be a revolutionary idea crucial for the development and evolution of England as a modern nation. Again, this was only proving that England was a nation ahead of its time. For the next several hundred years in England's history, this characteristic would hold true.

The War of the Roses

If it were not for the War of the Roses, then it could be asserted that the House of Tudor, the most famous and last royal dynasty of England before the country became a republic, would not have come to power. In 1455, a 32-year conflict between English noblemen and the English monarchy began. There are some people who believe that the ever-popular television show and book series *Game of Thrones* was based upon the War of the Roses, and while there were no dragons or fantastical white walkers in the real War of the Roses, there is a grain of truth in the foundation of both of these narratives. Both are concerning families feuding for a single crown; in the true historical case, this was the English crown. For years before the war officially began, two noble families had been in conflict regarding who was the most deserving of the English crown. The House of Lancaster and the House of York both claimed a direct descendant of the prior king of England, King Edward II, since both of them had come from King Edward II's sons.

Though the War of the Roses was initiated by the two families feuding for the English crown, it also set off a chain of events between other noble families who sided with either the House of York or the House of Lancaster. To recall from the earlier chapters, England was at war with France prior to and during the time of the War of the Roses. With funds being sent to the government to help supply the English military to fight against France, noble families were particularly invested in the best strategies to end the war. Since Richard of York, heading the House of York, and the House of Lancaster, headed by King Henry VI at the start of the War of the Roses, disagreed on tactics to end the war, other noble families joined the conflict based on their preferred strategy for the war with France. Throughout the 32 years that followed, the two families fought many brutal battles and performed a series of political manipulations on one another.

In 1455 at the Battle of St. Albans, one of the most famous battles of the war, the House of York took Henry VI prisoner, inciting a rebellion and retaliation from the House of Lancaster and giving temporary control of the crown over to Richard Neville of the House of York. King Richard maintained a fragile hand over the English crown while Henry VI's wife, Queen Margaret, worked secretly to secure her son's rightful place as the future heir. She built a remarkably well-equipped army in her husband's name and eventually sent them to battle with King Richard's army. The House of York won the battle, as well as the next several, capturing King Henry VI once again, while Queen Margaret continued to escape.

In 1460, with Henry under King Richard's bondage once more, King Richard convinced Henry to hand over the crown and end the fighting. Henry obliged, with the condition that he retain the crown until his death, at which point he would relinquish the English crown to the House of York. They signed the Act of Accord, but Queen Margaret was relentless in her desire to secure the throne. She prepared her army and sent it to fight King Richard's in retaliation for the Accord, killing Richard. When Richard's son, Edward, succeeded him, the bloodiest battle in the War of the Roses ensued at the battle of Towton, with 28,000 deaths recorded. As the Yorks won the battle and gained control of the crown, King Henry and Queen Margaret with their son ran to safety in Scotland.

While away, Queen Margaret garnered support from France and eventually ousted King Edward, restoring her husband to the throne in 1470. Soon after, with the death of King Henry, Queen Margaret, and their only son, King Edward returned to the throne. For several years, it appeared that the House of York had won, that is until Henry Tudor of the Lancastrian house saw his moment to take back the crown. Richard III, the king of England at the time of Henry Tudor's rebellion, was rumored to have been illegitimate and, therefore, unworthy of the crown. Henry Tudor seized his chance and gained assistance from France once more in fighting for the throne. He won and secured the English crown for the House of Lancaster, which quickly became the House of Tudors. The War of the Roses would find an organic and peaceful ending with the marriage of Henry and Elizabeth of York, ending the long conflict. With Henry's arrival to the throne, the Tudor Dynasty had begun.

The Tudors

The Tudor dynasty brought many changes to England, including a restructuring of the monarchy, the Church, and religious and social customs. In totality, the Tudors would rule England for 118 years, through five monarchs, including the famous King Henry VIII and Queen Mary I, the first female monarch in English history. King Henry VII did not last long on the throne, his marriage with Elizabeth bearing eight children, including his only surviving son Henry VIII.

When Henry VIII took the throne in 1509, England was officially entering a new era of unprecedented change. The second son in the Tudor family, Henry VIII was originally destined for a life in the clergy, but after being called to the throne out of necessity, the young king seemed born to rule and took to the newfound power quite naturally and willingly. Henry VIII brought a slew of changes to

England, the first and perhaps most famous one being that of the Church. Up until the 16th century, England had long been a Catholic country. The Church was a governing body all on its own and worked in tandem with the monarchy to devise the social and cultural structures of England. Henry VIII sought to change this, though, when his first wife, Catherine of Aragon, only bore him a daughter and no heir to the throne. Per the Catholic decrees, a man is to only take one wife, but Henry VIII created a loophole where there wasn't one before. With the supreme power of the English monarchy, Henry VIII rejected the Catholic Church and declared the Church of England, his own creation, the official religion of England. In this new religion, he was the overseeing power, not the Pope, and marriage was seen through a more flexible lens. Henry VIII annulled his marriage to Catherine of Aragon, a custom not recognized in Catholic traditions, and found himself a new wife in the venture to find an heir. After six other marriages, Henry VIII finally had himself a male heir.

While Henry VIII's creation of the Church of England allowed him to more freely make personal choices, benefiting him as an individual, it also altered England as a country on a broader spectrum. The Church of England, which would later be termed the Anglican Church, would eventually become the most popularly observed religion in England. It would also spread beyond Europe, reaching other countries, though none so completely as England itself. The religious change also altered the lives of common citizens. With the introduction of another church, suddenly religion was not quite as rigid as they'd initially believed it to be. The Church of England shared many values and customs with the Roman Catholic Church but differed, in that it adopted some of the ideals from the Protestant Reformation. It's considered more liberal in its beliefs and customs, allowing people more freedom within the customarily restrictive confines of religion.

Henry VIII also emphasized the importance of military prowess and introduced changes to the English Navy. He is colloquially termed "the Father of the English Navy," birthing the acclaimed navy that would prove nearly unstoppable in future conflicts and wars. When Henry VIII took the throne, he inherited a nearly nonexistent navy with only six ships. By the end of his reign, the Royal Navy had 60 ships, equipped and docked along England's shoreline, prepared for any imminent battle.

Today, the British Navy is regarded as one of the most formidable military organizations, next to the United States Military.

Henry VIII is perhaps one of the most famous Tudors, but he is only the first in the lineage of the Tudor dynasty that brought change to England. Henry VIII's only son, Edward, was king for only a brief time before he died, leaving the Tudor monarchy scrambling for a solution. Henry VIII left behind only daughters—Mary, his first daughter, and Elizabeth, his second—to take the throne. Henry VIII's firstborn, Mary, won her right to the throne, making history as the first female monarch.

As her first decree as queen, she reverted England back to Catholicism, disregarding her father's more democratic religion. If King Henry VIII's reign was shockingly progressive, then Queen Mary's reign was perilous in the name of tradition. A religious zealot, Queen Mary launched a campaign of religious persecution, executing over 300 Protestants (or as she termed them "heretics") during her reign and fracturing the religious sectors of England. It was through this crusade, known as the Marian persecutions, that Queen Mary earned her nickname "Bloody Mary," and rightly so. Even if

Queen Mary had not been a religious tyrant, she would have unfortunately still been disliked by the majority of the population, strictly on the basis of her gender. England was hesitant to embrace a female leader and, therefore, placed a greater emphasis on her marriage than they had on previous male monarchs. Upon Queen Mary's death, with no heirs to her name, she elected her younger sister, Elizabeth, as the new Queen of England, continuing the Tudor dynasty and enacting a kind of normalcy in recognizing a female as a possible monarch.

Queen Elizabeth I is heralded as one of the most successful monarchs in England's history, despite her rough introduction to the crown. A queen for 45 years, she was not welcomed as a new queen, facing similar discrimination as her sister had before her, with the addition of the scorched name of her mother, Anne Boleyn. Previous to King Henry VIII, children of anyone but the first wife were not considered prospects for the crown but rather "bastard children" who were not given any title or possibility of excelling in social spheres. Furthermore, Anne was also considered distanced from the crown and illegitimate due to Henry and Anne's divorce. With all of that being said, Queen Elizabeth I was the first to deny this tradition and slowly earned a great deal of respect from her subjects by turning England again toward prosperity. She returned England to its Protestant roots and welcomed a more free population. It was under her reign that the English Renaissance occurred, leaving citizens with an overwhelmingly positive perception of Queen Elizabeth I. Having watched the criticism her sister had endured as a female monarch, Queen Elizabeth I won a reputation as the "Virgin Queen" due to her reluctance to marriage, fearing that she would lose her power if she married a man into the monarchy.

It was under Queen Elizabeth I's rule that England became a colonial power. Queen Elizabeth I saw the importance of conquest and wanted to strengthen England's hold as an international power. Using the Royal Navy that her father created before her, Queen Elizabeth brought England into the conquest game. Sir Walter Raleigh was a favorite sailor and soldier of Queen Elizabeth I, making him an excellent candidate for the conquest missions she was devising. The Queen saw how the Spanish were beginning to sail out to new lands, claiming new colonies for their own, and how this might become a threat to England. Not one to be shown up, Queen Elizabeth sent her own ships out to discover new lands, one of the most famous and successful being Sir Walter

Raleigh's. If the name sounds familiar, it is most likely because it is tied to the colony of Roanoke, the "Lost colony." Though it has a rather disconcerting history, Roanoke was crucial in England's path to becoming a colonial power, marking it one of England's first (comparatively) successful colonies and paving the way for other conquests to come.

Since she never married, Queen Elizabeth I didn't have any heirs to her name. When she died after her long reign, the Tudor dynasty officially ended. With the closing of the Tudor dynasty, England would find itself turning toward a new age once again.

The Renaissance

Among all of the topics discussed in this book, the Renaissance is one of the most deserving of additional study. Entire college courses, entire tomes, are devoted to the Renaissance, making a brief introduction in a book of the entirety of English history fairly insubstantial in terms of understanding the Renaissance. As an overview of the period, it was commonly believed to be the era that ended the Middle Ages in England. The beginning of the Renaissance is debated, either starting with the Tudor dynasty or with the succession of Henry VIII to the English throne. Regardless, the height of the Renaissance took place during Elizabeth I's reign. Most of what people commonly learn about the Renaissance is actually specific to the Italian Renaissance. It's often identified as a time of artistic and scientific flourishing. When people think of the Renaissance, images of intricate paintings, inventions, and architectural feats come to mind. While this isn't untrue of the Renaissance, the English were having their own Renaissance in their own country.

While Italy flourished in terms of visual art, the English Renaissance saw a rebirth in terms of music and literature, giving way to famous writers such as John Donne, William Shakespeare, and John Milton. On the other end of the literary spectrum, William Tyndale published his new version of the Holy Bible, releasing the copy that would influence the King James Version, which is still the most widely used version of the Holy Bible to date.

Similar to the Italian Renaissance, the English Renaissance saw an emphasis on humanism, the belief in individuality and personal expression. This left room for English citizens to begin reimagining their lives as citizens, not just as English subjects. In terms of England's growth, it could be asserted that the

Renaissance was the nation's last hurrah in the era of childhood before entering adolescence. As people grew more satisfied with their personal lives and embraced the new morals of humanism, they also sought to better all other areas of their lives. Merchants began expanding trade routes, causing the English economy to flourish. With new inventions came new manufacturing systems, allowing for more efficient production and exportation. Political leaders began to reach out to other countries and attempt to make new alliances in the name of humanism.

Despite the prosperity that the English Renaissance brought, the era came to an end for a number of reasons. Some historians believe that the Counter-Reformation, or the Catholic Reformation, is to blame for ending the Renaissance, and in a country as traditionally Catholic as England, it is not such a feat to believe this. Coming out of the Renaissance, the Catholic Church sought to regain control, seeing humanism as a sinful rejection of the selfless nature of true, devout Christians. The Church began censoring artists again and preaching more widely about limiting one's self-expression in the name of piety. In 1545, the Council of Trent issued the Roman Inquisition, further pushing Renaissance ideals out of the picture. By the Church's decree, anyone exhibiting humanist ideals was punishable by death. Though there were also economic complications, with wars waging across the Italian peninsula throughout the 15th century, creating political instability at the end of the Renaissance, it was truly the Age of Enlightenment and the return to the Catholic Church's values that brought the Renaissance to an end. England would shift, yet again, as it entered the 17th century, finding new ways to fortify its growing kingdom and challenge itself as it continued to discover its place in the Western world.

CHAPTER 5

England and the "Age of Modernity"

As England moved into the 17th century, it was quickly becoming a kingdom proving itself as a modern and political power. They had begun colonies in the "New World," garnered a reputation for an unparalleled navy, and established a sense of stability under Queen Elizabeth I. They had made great advancements during their own Renaissance, where they flourished as an independent and humanist country, embracing what seemed to be the morals of the new modern world. But, as the Tudor dynasty ended, England was faced with a new monarchy, and with a new monarchy came new changes that brought civil unrest to the seemingly calm and united kingdom of England.

This era would also hold many changes for the neighboring countries of Scotland and Ireland.

For the foreseeable future, the history of both these nations was considered within the collective history of England, proving another unique quality of England. No other country considers another country's history also *their* history, but as time progressed, it would become more and more difficult to draw clear boundaries between the unified nations. In the 17th century, Ireland, Scotland, and England saw wars that led to direct impacts on the common people. Lands were confiscated from the poor, disease spread, and taxes skyrocketed. As it would come to pass, England's journey into the modern age was not one of peace or tranquility but of brutality and war. Though, it could be claimed that no passage, for a nation or an individual, into modernity is any other way.

English Civil Wars

After the death of Queen Elizabeth I, her cousin James Stuart, King James VI of Scotland, became the king of England and Ireland. The three kingdoms were united under one ruler for the first time in history, but the new rule would create a false sense of stability. While King James maintained some semblance of stability under his rule, it was when his son, Charles, took the throne that England would plunge into its first civil war. Charles wanted to use his sovereignty over Ireland, England, and Scotland to create a sort of uniformity among the nations. He began by instituting English religious doctrine in Scotland, which was met with resistance due to Scotland's Presbyterian population. Scotland met King Charles with their own forces, pushing him out of their country. King Charles turned to Parliament to supply him with the funds to retaliate against Scotland and pressure them into submitting to their rightful king. Parliament had been wary of King Charles since his assumption of the throne, though, and denied King Charles' request for funds, restricting the king's powers immediately. The disagreements between King Charles and Parliament continued when Ireland, currently under English rule, rebelled against England's Protestant population in Ireland, claiming that Ireland was traditionally a Catholic country and should remain as such. Parliament and King Charles disagreed, unsurprisingly, on how to react to the Catholics in Ireland, and King Charles eventually attempted to arrest five members of Parliament to prove his control over them. When Parliament discovered his power-hungry actions, King Charles feared that they would respond, and he fled to Northern England, signaling the official separation of Parliament and the monarchy for the first time since their alignment in England's early years. The civil war between those who aligned with Parliament and those who aligned with King Charles had begun.

In 1642, civil war broke out between the Royalist forces in the North and West and the Parliamentarians in the South and East. Initially, it appeared that the Royalists would win out in the first civil war, but when the Parliamentarians capitalized upon Scotland's rift with King Charles and allied with them, they gained invaluable support in the next wars to come. The Parliamentarians created what was called the New Model Army, with the help of their allies, and soon became unstoppable for the Royalists. In 1649, they captured, tried, and executed King Charles. For a time, England was under a Republican regime, but with King Charles' living son, Charles II, taking the throne of Scotland, he soon garnered military support to reclaim his father's English throne, resuming the civil war for himself.

The third civil war did not last long, considering the power that the Parliamentary forces had acquired over the years. King Charles II did not succeed in taking power away from Parliament and disbanding them, as his father had sought to do. Instead, Parliamentary forces defeated him, and King Charles II was forced to reconcile with Parliament, ending the third civil war and beginning the English Restoration.

Though the English civil wars did not end in significant political changes, as other wars had and would in the future, they left a hole in the population. By the end of the three civil wars, a total of 200,000 English civilians and soldiers had died, which, proportionate to the population of the time, is the equivalent of English lives lost in WWI. The English civil wars also showed England that while Parliament and the monarchy would work together to govern their kingdom, it was not always a cohesive relationship.

In 1660, with the return of King Charles II to the English throne, England began a gradual system of repairs to their political structures that had been damaged during the previous three civil wars. At this point in history, the three kingdoms—Ireland, England, and Scotland—were precariously linked and fragile in their political, economic, and social ties. Under King Charles II, Ireland, Scotland, and England were all united once more. To help sustain the newly united kingdoms, England expanded its trade once more and instituted a strict Anglican religious following, seeing it as the least divisive of the religions that had created a schism between the countries over the past several years. Unfortunately, the feelings of mistrust between Parliament and the English monarchy would not disappear but rather resurface again, less than 20 years later.

The Glorious Revolution: 1688–1689

The Glorious Revolution is termed such because technically no lives were lost and no physical battles fought during the conflict. It was, instead, a battle of manipulation and persistence between Parliament and the English crown to each gain more control over the other in the governance of England. King James II was crowned King of England in 1685, reigniting tensions between Parliament and the monarchy due to his staunch Catholic beliefs. Furthermore, he encouraged a general sense of freedom among the English population, suspended powers from Parliament, and appointed Catholic members to positions of great power in both political and military offices. King James continued to push his boundaries with Parliament when he married a Catholic woman, ensuring that the royal bloodline would remain Catholic even after King James passed. Parliament was disgruntled by this but sought to keep the peace with the monarchy. They invited King James for dinner to discuss a solution to their quarreling. The two came to an agreement that would forever change the governance of England.

Though a relatively short revolution, when compared to other wars in which England was involved, the Glorious Revolution had one of the most impactful endings of any war. Through the Glorious Revolution, England adopted the English Bill of Rights in 1689, which required that Parliament and the monarchy rule in a partnership while also placing some limitations on the crown. This was an invaluable change to England, and an unforeseen, but no less crucial, addition to the modern world. England was the first country to recognize that the ruling and governing powers needed limitations. Prior to this point in history, all rulers had governed their kingdoms with absolute oversight and unrestrained power. After the Glorious Revolution and the introduction of the English Bill of Rights, this pattern would change. The Glorious Revolution resulted in the cohesive partnership that is recognized today between Parliament and the English crown, a relationship that few countries have been able to replicate since. Even in modern times, countries would still be attempting to strike the balance between power and control of their governing

bodies.
Age of Enlightenment

Perhaps it could be asserted that Queen Elizabeth I's famous intellect and emphasis on education helped spur the Age of Enlightenment in England. She was venerated as a highly intelligent queen and strived to make a conscious and modern society that was not restricted by religious rules or hampered by past beliefs. She pointed England toward the future, and toward the future they moved. The Age of Enlightenment, also known as the "Age of Reason," spanned the 17th and 18th centuries in England, ushering in immense philosophical and intellectual developments that changed the country for the better. As the Renaissance had placed an emphasis on humanism, the Enlightenment encouraged people to seek out reason and structure. With the return to a stronger government, people started to shift their attention toward organization and understanding the smartest courses of action in all aspects of their lives. The unrest in their political and social spheres pushed people to consider solutions for themselves. Thinkers emerged out of the common population, eager to question and critique the systems in which they lived.

John Locke was one of the most famous thinkers to come from the English Enlightenment. Locke published many works during this time, all proclaiming that embracing human consciousness and reason was the only way for humans to truly be happy. He also wrote about the importance of the separation of church and state, which at the time, was a revolutionary way of thinking. Other thinkers also wrote during this time, such as Thomas Hobbes, who published his most famous work, *Leviathan*, which established some of the foundations of modern philosophy.

Outside of philosophy and political theory, England made significant scientific advancements under the new thinking. Education and logic were at the forefront of England's collective consciousness now, and famous scientists and inventors such as Nicholas Copernicus and Isaac Newton (not to mention Galileo, though he was not directly related to the English Enlightenment but rather the Italian one) were finally explaining how the universe worked. They were establishing the laws of the natural world, answering questions to which the Church had long been the only authority able to offer any explanation.

Out of the English Enlightenment, people

began to realize that their questions could have answers and their world was vast but understandable, at least. With logic and education, people could finally understand what had once seemed so unreachable, it was supernatural or divine in its vastness. Without the Enlightenment, areas of study such as chemistry, astronomy, and the social sciences would not exist. Prior to the Enlightenment, there had not been a reason to study one's past or question one's present. As a kingdom, England was taking steps toward its place as the leader of the modern world.

CHAPTER 6

Georgian England

The 18th century in England was one predominantly of transition. The English crown was passing from one monarchy to the other, starting the long line of Georges on the English throne. Political parties within England were strengthening their holds and even extending overseas. As England had devoted much of the 17th century to spreading its roots and becoming a colonial power, they would pay the price for their endeavors in the 18th century. Their colonies would gather confidence and rise up against the now-great British empire, resulting in one of the most successful revolutions in the world: The American Revolution. Unsurprisingly, the famous King George of the revolution is part of this era, which left a permanent stamp on the culture and history of England. The 18th century would force England to test its new boundaries as a kingdom and as a powerful empire with seemingly limitless boundaries. By the end of the century, there would be no question that England was a powerful player in the modern world, having sown the very seeds that would grow into the United States.

On a moral and social level, the Georgian era for England would sew new oats of nationalism and patriotism. The English would continue to hone their pride for their country. The acclaimed *Encyclopedia Britannica*, a resource that is digitized now and still in use today, saw its first publication during the Georgian era and introduced to citizens and scholars alike the first glimpse of what their country really had to offer to the world. During this time, England maintained what is perhaps its most famous culture and society. It was a unique combination of brutality (both military and civilian) and classical literature, art, and customs. The English would continue this balance of strict civility and organic barbarism for the next several hundred years.

Jacobite Rebellion

Following on the heels of the Glorious Revolution, in the early days of the 18th century, a new rebellion would begin in England. The common people predominantly of Scotland were displeased with the current English monarchy and the outcome of the Glorious Revolution. The Jacobite Rebellion of the 18th century was actually the second Jacobite rebellion, but of the two it was the more successful one in achieving the united goals of both movements. When the first Jacobite rebellion broke out in 1689, it was following the newly appointed English monarchs, William and Mary. William of Orange and Mary II had been selected by the English to serve on the throne instead of James II, who had originally been in line to rule. James II was a Catholic, and the English (ever the wary travelers of the realm of religion) were concerned that his ruling might lead to another Catholic uprising. Thus, they removed him from the throne and promptly replaced him with William and Mary, who were Protestants. But England did not take into account that they were now united with Scotland, an overwhelmingly Catholic country. Those who supported James II and wanted him, or at least the Stuart dynasty, restored to the throne termed themselves the Jacobites and rose up against the monarchy.

The first Jacobite uprising was fairly unsuccessful, ending in flaccid battles, James II's return to France, and a failed renewal of his status as the English and Scottish monarch.

Starting in the 1690s and continuing on through 1715, the second Jacobite uprising was built on a continued dissatisfaction with King William and poor living conditions for those in Scotland. They wanted change, and they believed a new monarch would be the answer to their Catholic prayers. This rebellion would end with the return of Anne Stuart to the throne as well as Hanoverian armies beating the Jacobites.

The Jacobites would have two more uprisings. The third would be instigated by the Spanish in the hopes that civil unrest would help them reclaim land they had lost to the English in the War of Spanish Succession. This attempt to overthrow the English crown would falter as well, resulting in thousands of lost Spanish soldiers and no movement on the English crown. The final uprising was not a victory for the Jacobites, but it did result in political changes to protect the English government against them. The Jacobites had earned such a name for themselves across Europe as ruthless, power-hungry rebels who would stop at nothing to attain victory. Unfortunately, it also contributed to a long-standing hatred for the Gaelic culture and any people living in the Scottish Highlands. The English Parliament instituted several precautions to act against possible or confirmed Jacobites. In 1746,

Parliament passed the Disarming Acts, which outlawed any representation of Gaelic culture. In addition, they passed a forfeiture of land owned by any Jacobite, robbing them of all livelihood after the rebellions.

The Jacobite Rebellions eventually had a negative effect on the very Scottish Highlanders who had started it in the first place. By the time their rebellions had been stamped out, their entire way of life was snuffed out with it. It would also create a reputation for the Scottish people that would stain the country as a whole. That being said, the minor success of the Jacobite Rebellions was in aiding the future restoration of the Stuart dynasty to the English crown. Their success would swing wide the doors of the 18th century in England.

Acts of Union

To be clear, England had been endeavoring to unite itself with other countries prior to the 16th century. In fact, all the way back in 1284, the English crown annexed Wales, which in effect, gave England power over Wales but didn't necessarily incorporate Wales into the kingdom as a whole. This more complete incorporation of Wales into England wouldn't happen until 1536 with King Henry VIII's Act of Union. Once this was passed, the Welsh people would be given the same rights and laws as those in England. Wales was also granted positions in Parliament, expanding the idea of equal representation and taking the first step of many toward turning England into the United Kingdom. In 1603, with Queen Elizabeth's death and her cousin James I's ascension to the throne, England and Scotland became unified under the same crown, as King James had already been the king of Scotland since 1567. Though it was his goal to unify the two nations, he only accomplished this in a symbolic sense. England created a new flag featuring both the English and Scottish crosses, more commonly known as the "Union Jack." The flag was the forerunner to the flag of the United Kingdom, which would come with the next Act of Union.

In 1702, Anne Stuart, the sister of the last king and queen, inherited the English throne, temporarily returning England to the Stuart dynasty. Queen Anne's rule was short but crucial in forming the political sphere of modern England. At the beginning of the century, Scotland was in dire need of economic assistance. In return, England was concerned that Scotland might serve as a neutral pass-through for France to launch attacks on England. The two sought a symbiotic solution, and unification seemed to be the simplest answer. Scotland was forced to reconcile its parliament but remained able to maintain its system of laws. This would prove problematic in the future, but for the time being, the two countries saw a manageable agreement. In May 1707, a new Act of Union was passed, combining England and Scotland into the United Kingdom. Anne Stuart would serve as monarch for both countries, and Parliament would be the governing body for them as well. As time went on, the United Kingdom would grow more, but the first step had at least been taken. England was nurturing a new side of itself with this decision. Not only was the nation willing to maintain strong trade and political relationships with other countries, but England was also finally prospering enough to, in essence, take another country under its wing and consider it part of its own kingdom.

Political Parties

With England evolving as a kingdom, its political sphere was expanding with it. Within England, two predominant political parties were emerging, an idea that perhaps had existed for centuries but had yet to gain enough strength and commitment to earn a structural shift. It was during the Georgian period that the Whigs and the Tories, the political parties that would eventually follow to America, emerged in

England. During the previous disagreements concerning James II's rise to the throne, the names came as derogatory labels for the opposing sides. In a sense, then, we have the Jacobite Rebellion to thank, too, for England's most prominent political parties. Those who supported James II were given the name "Tory," an Irish term for "papist outlaw," due to their belief in James' lineage as a Roman Catholic on the throne. On the opposing side were the "Whigs," a Gaelic name that indicates thievery. The term was applied to the Scottish Presbyterians for their attempts to steal the throne, as the English considered it.

Though the names were applied to indicate groups that supported or were against the monarchy, they remained even after the conflicts between the Jacobites and the English. It was under Queen Anne's rule that the political parties developed their own connotations. The Whigs became associated with the resistance, a group of people who were in support of Anglicanism and the nobles. They were against the monarchy and were often associated with religious dissent. Tories, on the other hand, were linked to aristocracy. They were more traditional and in support of maintaining the customs that England had established over the past centuries. They were opposed to religious toleration and any foreign affairs that challenged the current state of England.

The impact of these parties would prove especially resounding in the coming years as England faced its most formidable ally and enemy yet. Their own colony, America, would rise up against them to earn its independence, and it was partially these original political groups that would be to blame for the arguments that spurred the revolution. Both the Whigs and the Tories would make it across the Atlantic to the new colony, bringing with them the opinions of their past parties as well as evolving within the political and social climates of their new environment.

The American Revolution

Overwhelmingly, it is the American War of Independence, or the American Revolution, that served as the most altering event of the 18th century, both in England and America. In the 17th and 18th centuries, England had devoted itself to leading the colonization movement in which Spain, Portugal, and France were all involved. While Spain and France soon pulled ahead with England, as the 18th century progressed, it was clear that these three would reign supreme in the efforts to conquer foreign lands. Spain and France had an ulterior motive for conquering lands though: Profit. They conquered lands for the exports that would lend themselves to their respective countries, giving them valuable trade materials that other countries didn't have. As a result, their territories were less colonies and more business franchises. England had more domestic aspirations for their conquests, hoping to spread their kingdom as widely as possible across the quickly expanding "known" world. They claimed land and quickly set to colonizing it, establishing homes and businesses. They looked at colonies as extensions of themselves and less as business ventures. It is true that they took many valuable assets from their new-world colonies, but at the heart of their colonization effort was a desire to have English touchstones across the globe: In essence, to make the country of England borderless and their presence ubiquitous. This strategy, while proving beneficial, would eventually backfire for the English. Their colonists were too self-sufficient, their establishments too successful. In an effort to create lives outside of England, the English soon found that the extension of themselves wanted a severing, and the amputation would be bloody.

Similar to the Renaissance, entire tomes and college courses have been devoted to the

American Revolution. It is a complex war that involved a litany of battles and pivotal events on both sides of the conflict. To begin, the main incentive for the revolution could be clearly seen as the independence of England's 13 colonies grew. Colonists were developing a disinterest in and distaste for England. They felt distanced from the country, both culturally and physically, and were angered by the continued governance of their affairs by an authority to which they no longer felt connected. Tensions had been building between the colonies and England for years before war broke out in 1775. England had gained new territories in the French and Indian War, but with new territories came new expenses. England enforced new taxes on the colonists to help pay for their future plans of expansion and colonization. With the Stamp Act, Townshend Act, and infamous Tea Act, colonists were feeling economically strapped by a country they were growing to detest. England sensed their unease and stationed British soldiers in the colonies to help enforce the tax collections and keep the peace. With tensions rising, it took only a single match to light the fire at the Boston Massacre in 1770, the first of many conflicts between the two sides.

Both the colonists and the English knew that they could not simply shrug off the Boston

Massacre, and England sent more troops to the colonies. The colonists responded by creating more conflict. The famous Boston Tea Party was yet another act against the English, followed shortly after in 1774 by the first Continental Congress meeting. American leaders, such as George Washington, John Adams, and Samuel Adams, as well as many others, met to discuss a formal disintegration of the bonds between England and the colonies. England, a powerful kingdom that had fought hard for its borders to extend across the sea would not stand for this insurrection, though, and sent troops to stop the war of independence before it could begin. With the acclaimed "shot heard round the world," when British troops landed and fought the first battle against waiting American troops, the American Revolution began.

Several more battles would ensue in the first years of the revolution, but it was the political game that America played that cost England their most successful colonies. The American Revolution would further capitalize on the discrepancies and history of unease between England and France. Being former English subjects themselves, or at least descendants of them, the American colonists were well aware of the tumultuous history that England had with France. The two were constantly at odds, and the colonists sought to use this to their advantage by allying with the French, a military and political decision that would help to solidify their eventual victory. Americans also drew from England's history of historical documents and its people's own pleas for independence in order to create the Declaration of Independence, inspired by England's Magna Carta as well as its integration of the parliamentary system to establish more equal representation by the nation's own people.

After eight years of battles and political manipulation, England had to formally recognize America's status as a free country with the signing of the Treaty of Paris in 1783. England also had to sign peace treaties with Spain and France, who had entered the war to support the Americans, though more so to see the English finally defeated. While the American Revolution was heralded as a victory for America, it signaled a change in England. It showed the English that in their effort to create an expansive kingdom, they would have to monitor their colonies closely. Ownership, they saw, was not permanent. Their people had minds of their own, and England could not act as an overbearing parent forever, as they would later see with other colonies.

CHAPTER 7

Victorian England

The Victorian era in England's history is overwhelmingly recognized as its most prosperous and overall productive period. England made leaps and bounds in terms of economic prosperity and political gain. It extended its colonial powers, asserting itself as the head of international colonial efforts. It expanded its boundaries, became the parent of the greatest success story that colonies would look to for generations, and was in a solid place to build cultural and intellectual progress. The Victorian era only earned its name from the era's monarch, Queen Victoria, who played a major part in shaping England's future. It was during the Victorian era that England saw some of the most intellectual and academic advancements that the world had ever seen since ancient Greece. It was a time for English citizens to prosper, but it was also a tipping point for England. They were at a crossroads, politically speaking, and they were entering the age of Imperialism. As a country with a longstanding history of being an imperial power, England had a reputation to uphold as more countries entered the race to colonize the globe. They also had learned valuable lessons from the American Revolution and would take these into the new century. England would undergo yet more change during the Victorian era, emerging, as they hoped, stronger and more prepared for what the 20th century would bring.

The Victorian era was also characterized by a class-based society. This meant that England was modernizing in a way that it hadn't before. In previous centuries, feudalism had either reigned supreme as the governing societal structure, or it had hung on, enduring longer than most would have preferred. Entering the Victorian era, power was organized differently. Power was no longer based strictly on titles but corresponded to wealth, meaning the more wealth and property someone had, the more power they had. This opened the doors for the majority of the English population who had previously been barred from advancing in society. This idea of freedom for every man would ring true in many different areas of people's lives. More people would earn the right to vote in this era, and cultural restrictions would break as well, giving people an overall less restrictive way of life.

The English Government in Victorian Times

Prior to Queen Victoria taking the throne at the age of only 18, the longest-reigning monarch was King George III. King George III had reigned as ruler of England, Ireland, and eventually the United Kingdom from 1760 to 1820. Today, he is still the longest-reigning king of England. But Queen Victoria was not one to be shown up. She assumed the throne after King George IV and King William IV. When she took the throne in 1837, the kingdom was at a political tipping point. They had recovered from the American Revolution but now turned their sights inward to build a strong country from within. In 1837, Queen Victoria inherited the first year of the smallpox epidemic in England. This would only be the first bump in the road of her 63-year reign of England.

Queen Victoria was incredibly popular among the common people, and this would bode well for her as the position of the English monarchy changed drastically during her reign. Political parties were shifting during Queen Victoria's era. The two original parties, the

Whigs and the Tories, still maintained their statuses in England, but as the culture was changing, so did they. The parties wanted to shed their old values and names for new, evolved characteristics and classifications. As such, the Tories became the Liberals and the Whigs eventually became the Conservatives, though still favoring aristocratic ideals. The change was made in an effort to survive throughout the rest of the political changes that would take place during the Victorian era. Perhaps it was an assertion of their expectation that they would need to appeal more directly to Parliament in the coming years. Those associated with political parties recognized early that the attachment to the English monarchy and the real power that Parliament held was shifting; showing direct ties to the old monarchy and the old ways might not serve them in the future.

Despite Queen Victoria's appeal to the common man during her reign, the House of the Lords (the English monarchy) was overshadowed by the House of Commons (Parliament). It was at this point that England was turning toward an even more modernized country, one that was beginning to recognize the old ways of a governing monarchy less and less. Suddenly, Queen Victoria turned into a symbol of the country, rather than a sole governing head. At this time, Parliament held immense power, also reflecting the social changes in England that emphasized representation more and more. It included 600 members who had been elected by the public to represent England, Ireland, Wales, and Scotland. Victorian England may have been named after its monarch, but it earned much of its political progress through the strengthening of its parliament.

Imperial Era

The English people had developed a sense of pride over the imperial nature of their country. England was not simply a kingdom strong within itself. It expanded across the globe, and by the 20th century, it would cover over one fifth of the earth's land surface. The British people acknowledged that they were superior to other countries in their political and cultural advancements. Though it could be argued that all citizens feel this way about their country, the English had a certain level of responsibility to this emotion. They were entitled to a feeling of superiority since their country had proven itself, again and again, as a kingdom that would continue to rise, despite each challenge they faced. Coming out of the 18th century, England was eager to continue in the race to conquer the rest of the globe and discover new territories.

At the start of the 19th century, England won victory against France in the Napoleonic wars, resulting in a strengthening of their Navy and an assertion that they were a superior empire. With their newfound strength, they went on to colonize areas in Asia, Africa, and the Pacific Islands. They experienced a period of peace in which, although they were fighting other countries in an arms race, so to speak, they weren't necessarily in any wars. Once islands in the Pacific and countries in Africa were conquered, England's trade exploded. England was at the peak of an indefatigable economy, pushing out more goods and balancing more wealth than it ever had before. The first World's Fair in 1851 was a celebration of this prosperity, showcasing all of the foreign goods that England had obtained and been trading with the world. Upon conquering India, England obtained what was often referred to as "the jewel in the kingdom's crown," as it served to be one of their most profitable sources of exports. When England, Spain, and France turned to Africa, they divided up the continent for each country. This opened wide the slave trade for England, expanding it from what it already had been generations prior. England also overtook areas in South America, Australia, the Caribbean, and China.

Industrial Revolution

England's working class and their sources of industry were areas that changed the most during this era. Though that may seem like an extreme evaluation, it is true when considering that it was England who arrived at the Industrial Revolution first. England's industrial revolution would serve as an inspiration and a foundation on which America would build theirs 50 years later. Though the end result of the Industrial Revolution served to benefit England tenfold, the events preceding it, which necessitated the industrialization of the country's economy, were incredibly taxing on the people.

In the early part of the 19th century, England and its longtime partner, Ireland, saw great famines sweep the nations. In England, the 1840s were known as "The Hungry Forties," during which poverty and famine skyrocketed in England. Despite the overall prosperity in England's Victorian period, in 1839, they suffered a dip in economic trade, which put a strain on the economy that had grown accustomed to prospering over the past several years. With trade down, there was less money circulating in the economy, and all areas were affected. England suffered poor harvests for the next several years, which coupled with the increasing population (as a result of the initial success of England's new era) were a recipe for economic disaster. In 1845, a potato blight came to England and Scotland, further intensifying the costs of famine across both countries. Then, in the following year it spread to Ireland, ultimately leading to the Great Potato Famine, one of Ireland's most defining historical events.

When England emerged out of these hard times, the people knew that they needed to re-evaluate their economy. Coupled with the developing feelings of independence, freedom, and personal ingenuity among the social classes, the English took it upon themselves to industrialize their economy. Railroads and steamships expanded their routes, spreading farther than they ever had before. With an increase in transportation options, England could not only increase their imports, protecting them from any future famines that would limit them to their own resources, but they could also increase the customers available to them for their own exports. This brought new money into the economy, re-invigorating it. The electric telegraph had been invented in 1837, and soon England began to implement that as well, drawing the borders of their large world closer.

The most recognizable additions of industrialization were also prevalent in

England. They shifted from incremental, worker-based economies to industries based out of factories. They changed the training of workers from teaching them trades to teaching them a single aspect of a trade. No more were there cobblers but, instead, 50 people who knew how to make the shoelaces and another 50 who could make the soles. Their economy exploded, but their living standards failed to catch up. America would face the same challenges in the next century with its own industrial revolution, in which economy and capitalism were placed over the well-being of the worker. Furthermore, England's population was increasing exponentially during the Victorian era, going from 13 million to 32 million, and these numbers didn't include immigrants who were coming to England themselves in hopes of having a better life. The population sought jobs in factories, earning very little, but providing the backbone for a booming economy that bolstered elites at the top of society who were becoming increasingly wealthy in this new era.

Intellectual Accomplishments

Britain was the capital of the English-speaking world, making it the center of culture during the Victorian era. England, or at least its citizens, seemed to be well aware of this and did not fail to take leaps and bounds in the literary world. The Victorian era saw a revolution within itself within the world of the humanities and the arts. England brought forth new types of poetry, music, theater, and fiction and nonfiction prose. In the intellectual realm, it would be sufficient to claim that England did not suffer during the Victorian era. It was during this era that England earned its most prominent writer, short of Shakespeare: Charles Dickens. Dickens had such a lasting impact on England, and the world at large, that England would earn its own nickname for the era in which he wrote and the portrayals that he painted of his country: Dickensian England. Charles Dickens wrote incredibly long novels, later termed "Victorian novels" that relied more on common stories of people's lives rather than fables or religious tales of the past. It was his novels that popularized the form of serial publication that other Victorian novels would rely on later.

The Victorian era brought an increase in education and general intellect, and with the booming economy, more people had more money to gain access to what they had previously been restricted from. Literacy rates improved in this era, and now that more money was circulating, nearly every person in Britain could afford to read. What had once been a luxury for only the elite was now becoming knowledge afforded to the common man. Publishers caught on to this and tried to popularize reading, capitalizing on the wider population now available to them. They began printing serial publications, monthly installments of full-length novels, that were more widely distributed and cheaper for the common public. Dickens' novels, a popular favorite of the time, paved the way for other authors, like William Thackeray and Lewis Carroll, to publish in such a way. Other writers began publishing novels that fell into a different category, a new one altogether: Gothic novels. Along with Edward Hyde and Dracula, we also have the Victorian Age to thank for Sherlock Holmes.

Soon, the English population was not only widely literate, but they were also actively engaged in the support of their own modern culture through literature. England was bringing the arts out of the elite and into the popular sphere, creating a more equal and all-around enlightened population.

In addition to fiction prose, there was a change in poetry as well. Poets relied less on the rising literacy rates and more on the shifting political and moral beliefs of the majority. The Victorian era gave rise to the first wave of modern poetry. Poets began writing with an emphasis on the senses, publishing more passionate poems than had populated the canon previous to the Victorian era. Poets also began taking more risks with the style and content of their poems. One of the most famous poets of this period, who capitalized on these characteristics of the changing genre, was Alfred, Lord Tennyson.

Nonfiction writers in the Victorian era were not to be left out. There are two areas within the concentration that perhaps left the most lasting impact on not only English culture but the cultures of all countries: Journalism and science writing. The Victorian era saw the wave of "New Journalism" come crashing in, drawing on the sensational qualities of news reporting. Journalists were quickly becoming entertainers and not just informers of the truth. In fact, it was at this time that England paved the way for all journalism to come that would no longer simply report the facts but would attempt to tell a story that would make people want to continue reading. Furthermore, one of the most widely read books, a lifelong project that still continues today, was first started in the Victorian era: *The Oxford English Dictionary*.

Last, but not least, it would be a cataclysmic

oversight to omit Charles Darwin and his *On the Origin of Species* from this overview of Victorian history. Darwin released his most famous book in 1859, though he had been a scientist and travel writer for 20 years prior to that. Darwin published his book during the Victorian era, hoping that with the influx of intellectual thought and academic emphasis, it might be more welcomed. People were embracing the necessity of understanding one's world and welcomed the new ways of the artistic and political environments with open arms. Science, however, has always been an area of hesitance and concern. His book questioned the very origin of our human race, staking his claim on years of studying evolution, both of humans and apes, finches, and other mammals that helped him to devise revolutionary theories. He posed the evolution theory, throwing a wrench not only in the common person's assumptions of their origins but in the Church's theories about humans' existence. Darwin's book set off a chain of reactions from both scientific and religious leaders. People were reluctant to believe his theories, though today they are heralded as revolutionary. It is perhaps fair to assume that, despite the progressive ideals of the Victorian era, Darwin's *On the Origin of Species* was ahead of its time, becoming the most influential academic book in 2015.

CHAPTER 8

The World at War

Despite everyone's best efforts, no country was quite prepared for the 20th century. Nor was any country quite prepared for just the *first half* of the 20th century. England entered the 20th century as a declining empire. It had reached its peak during its imperial era, mostly overlapping with the Victorian era, and was now facing the challenges of coexisting with other modern countries in a modern world. England was not the only one on the map anymore, and other countries like France, Germany, and the United States were vying for supreme power. England would be underprepared in terms of military development as it entered the 20th century. Though the English had spent the last 50 years dominating the colonization scene, they had overlooked military advancements, leaving themselves with a scant number of military troops.

Socially speaking, they were amending some of the wrongs that they had sewn during the Industrial Revolution. England was instituting social reforms to improve the quality of life of the common population, who were predominantly overworked and underpaid for their labor. England worked to institute work reforms to improve conditions and give their workers rights. They were also implementing education changes to improve the overall quality of their intellectual population. The Victorian era had set the stage for a well-educated and enlightened English population, and the 20th century would build on this foundation.

Politically, England was struggling with the steady reduction of the power of its traditional monarchy. In 1909, the Liberal Party passed the Parliament Act, denying monarchs the right to veto any financial bills. This was further emphasizing the changing role of the English monarch. The modern world was one fit for a parliament, not a single power, and England was slowly embracing it. Women were vying for the right to vote, latching onto the growing sense for equal representation that seemed to be spreading across the country. Their efforts, along with any and all social reform, would be halted in 1914 with the start of World War I.

As the world left behind the Victorian era, countries moved toward progress. Economic, social, and cultural shifts abounded. The Industrial Revolution in England established a new society, one driven by progress and permanently linked to other countries. Trade and colonial ties had always been intrinsic to England as a country, but as they entered the new 20th century, they began to realize that it was not simply trade that connected countries. International relationships were quickly becoming dictating factors within each country. It would eventually become more and more apparent that a single country's actions did not occur within a vacuum. As the world grew, the magnetism between each border and the relationships among each nation grew tighter and tighter.

Though there are many different theories as to just how the First World War began, there is no argument regarding England's involvement in its development. England would prove its military and social prowess during the war years. Its economic and social systems would be tested, but throughout the next 40 years of England's history, the nation would be challenged and emerge as one of the world's key power players.

The First World War: 1914–1918
The Beginning

Germany was England's unforeseen enemy as they entered the 20th century. In the 19th century, England had focused on a political policy known as "splendid isolation" in which it placed its efforts on strengthening its European kingdom. The English had their sights set on an unstoppable United Kingdom and were striving to make this a reality. Unfortunately, as England realized at the beginning of the 20th century, this left them exposed and vulnerable to other countries outside of Europe. In the first 10 years of the 20th century, England laid the groundwork to repair this misstep. They signed the Anglo-Japanese Alliance in 1902 and the 1904 Entente Cordial with France; in 1907, they attended the Anglo-Russian Convention that allowed England to expand their navy and other military efforts. It also established a cordial relationship with Russia, who seemed to be the closest with Germany, the rising threat in the early 20th century.

Germany was expanding their navy, which attracted England's attention immediately. England had an established, centuries-long reputation for having the strongest navy, so when Germany began building more ships and adding to their naval reserves, England's concern was sparked. England watched as Germany was quickly becoming a military powerhouse. They had a history of choosing military conquest before moral appeals when dealing with other countries, and England was well aware of this. In 1911, after the Agadir Crisis involving French and German troops and naval ships, England and France began secret negotiations to discuss the possibility of Germany beginning a war in Europe. Their once age-old rivalry would prove to become the most lasting and vital partnership in the wars to come.

Some historians believe that it was England's apprehension concerning Germany's military expansion that caused them to enter the war. Others are more convinced that it was actually Germany's booming economy that England saw as a threat that should be expelled. Others still believe that it was actually England's loyalty to France that brought them into World War I. When Germany invaded Belgium in 1914, England was afraid of history repeating itself. In 1870, German and Prussian states obliterated France, and their military had only strengthened since then. England was afraid that if the Germans continued to push across France, they would reach the English Channel, gaining control of one of their most vital trade routes. England couldn't let France be defeated again and place itself in an economically vulnerable position that would require its involvement in a new war.

The reasons for World War I beginning—in other words, the spark that lit the fire—are still undecided and debated among academic circles constantly. The most popular and widely circulated story of the beginning of WWI is told through the lens of the assassination of Archduke Ferdinand by a Serbian rebel, causing a schism in Austria-Hungary and Serbian relations. Russia and Germany came to the aid of each region as support split down party lines. Russia supported Austria-Hungary, and Germany supported Serbia. Here entered the concern about the state of France as Germany was escalating its military presence, along with England's concern about looking overly self-centered or too concerned with its own problems within its own borders. The theory of England wanting to come to France's aid and getting caught in the crossfire was true, but what also weighed heavily on Britain's government was the consequences of its previous century of isolation. The world was not one of isolation anymore but one of support and integration, and England needed to show that it was willing to support this turn of the modern world. Furthermore, on a more selfish and economic note, England needed to protect its oil investments in Iran. If Germany gained too much power, they could overthrow the British presence in Iran and take the oil supplies for themselves.

When Germany invaded Belgium, England officially declared war on August 4, 1914, claiming that its entrance into the war was due to the protections required of the nation by the Treaty of London, while safeguarding its more political incentives. The declaration of war on Germany required the support of every dominion, colony, and protection of the United Kingdom, meaning that even though Britain declared war, it was certainly more than just English citizens and the English government that were involved in this first world war.

War, Terrible War

Again, World War I is another topic to which entire books, college courses, and scholars' lives are devoted to studying. World War I was monumental in bringing the world, including England, into the modern violence and political games of the 20th century. It ushered in a new kind of world, one that required the kind of strength, on the political and civilian level, that countries had never had to supply. It introduced modern warfare, tactics that soldiers had never used before. Coming off the heels of the Industrial Revolution, many countries were utilizing technology that they themselves didn't understand. With a combination of modern technology and outdated tactics, World War I was one of the deadliest conflicts in history and, in fact, *the* deadliest war the world had seen thus far. It would not be surpassed until World War II, though in some ways it was more gruesome even than that.

England's involvement in World War I was fairly absolute. They ran political games as well as contributed soldiers to the fronts that sprang up all across France. With the start of the war, countries chose sides, falling into either the Central powers (mainly comprised of Germany and Austria-Hungary) or the Allied powers (the United Kingdom, Japan, Italy, Russia, and the United States). Immediately facing Germany's unparalleled military powers, England realized that it needed to re-evaluate its military. World War I brought many changes to England, but the most obvious military advancement was the creation of the British Air Force. Airplanes were an innovation from the last century, but with the new type of warfare of the 20th century, they were now being utilized for military conquest.

As British and French forces fought German forces in the early years of the war, England strived to continue to make advancements with their military technology. They were engaged in trench warfare, the well-known stalemate tactic of the First World War. Both sides had found themselves at a stalemate for months before England took another step forward in modern warfare and introduced the first tank to the battlefield. The first tanks were dangerous and difficult to maneuver, but it was, at least, a step in the direction of military evolution on England's part. It would continue to advance as years went by, the First World War being only a rough introduction.

World War I was the first time that England had ever been truly affected on its home front by a war. Previously, it had been successful in keeping wars in other countries or maintaining a stronghold at its borders, but with the integration of aerial warfare, the English found themselves in what was called "total warfare." Civilians were being bombed in their home country, transforming how the British people began to think about war. No more was it something that occurred outside of their homes, and even their country. In the new world, it was a matter of daily concern and fear, invading every aspect of people's lives. In this same vein, the newspapers that had been revamped during the Victorian age sought to help the war effort as well. Wartime propaganda was a major asset during World War I and would remain a tool for governments during wartime for every war following it. Under total warfare, all avenues were geared toward supporting the war effort, especially the manufacturing and factory businesses. The workforce turned toward the war, changing what they manufactured, how they manufactured, and who was allowed to work. As the war went on and the number of casualties continued to steadily rise, English men began enlisting to replenish the troop numbers and to fulfill their duty to their country. But with all of the men going off to war, someone had to maintain industries on the homefront. In this way, World War I is sometimes credited with letting women into the mainstream workforce, changing the standards that the British held for equality concerning gendered careers. Women earned jobs wherever they could to help support the war effort, keeping the country running while their men fought in the terrible war. Eventually, World War I became too consuming to keep women on the home front. Though it took some political shifting, by the end of the war almost 80,000 women had joined the armed forces as nurses or cooks, breaking the staunch barrier between them and the military. Both civilians and troops were heavily impacted by the war. By the end of World War I, military deaths were said to have risen above 850,000, while the civilian death rate surpassed that of both the Spanish flu and previous famines. It was by no means a low number though, considering that while civilians died of malnutrition from war rationing, they were also hit with the Spanish flu in 1918 and lost the lives of more innocent people.

Though it may appear on the surface that England was a united front at home, such was not the case. In the Victorian era, while England experienced immense wealth and prosperity, it drew thousands of immigrants to the country. Previously, it had been a sign of England's success as a nation to stabilize itself enough to attract citizens of other countries. But when World War I broke out, it was soon seen as a threat by many English citizens. In August of the first year of the war, Parliament passed the Aliens Restriction Act, which required all foreign immigrants who had come to England to register with the police and the government. By the next year, almost 70,000 German, Hungarian, and Austrian immigrants had registered. England claimed it was a way to keep track of the immigrant population, but really it was a reflection of their mistrust of the "enemy" in their own country. Registered citizens of other countries were restricted on their travel plans and what merchandise they could purchase, and their homes could be searched at any time. As anti-German sentiment rose across the nation, England soon started interning foreign citizens. Although, by 1915 with the sinking of the Lusitania, such attitudes had peaked and would only decrease as the war went on.

The Aftermath

The first turning point in World War I that swung the war in the direction of the Allied powers was the arrival of American troops to Europe. After the sinking of the Lusitania, America arrived in Europe in 1917 to join the Allied powers. Though America's contribution during WWI on the ground was actually quite minimal, their presence gave the appearance to the German forces that the Allied powers had infinite troops who could be mobilized at any time and transported anywhere. This was understandably intimidating to Germany and helped to sink their morale. The second turning point of the war was in 1918 when German forces attacked too quickly, depleting their forces substantially in the Battle of the Marne.

Finally, when Allied forces finally crossed the Hindenburg Line on the Western Front, forcing German troops to retreat, it was only a short time until November when Germany, depleted of goods and troops, had to call an armistice to end the war.

The impact of World War I on England and the world at large is undeniable. Germany's territory was minimized exponentially, and its economy was quickly depleted with the enforcement of reparations to France for the war. This would eventually impact England as Germany turned back to them in WWII for supporting the peace treaty that required reparations. England's economy was also heavily taxed from the war. They had gone from being the leading economy of the world to one of the largest debtors. It had also led to political changes, as many people turned to support the Labour Party, replacing the previously established Liberal Party, which had been strong going into the war. However, the largest impact on England was by far a psychological one. The English had believed themselves a proud, unstoppable country, but by the end of World War I, they had been extremely humbled. With their social structures shaky and their economy on the mend, they would turn to the only standing country that had emerged from

World War I on the upside: The United States.

The Interwar Years: 1918–1939

Between the two world wars, England attempted to catch its breath. England would undergo more political changes within its bodies of government. They would undergo the same Great Depression that crushed other countries around the world, and although it would not have the same detrimental effects on England as other places, England would no doubt be affected. What categorized the interwar years as crucial for England was a transformation after the Great War. England took the time after World War I not only to recover from its losses in all areas of life but, in a sense, to start anew. Activism for women's rights as well as the treatment of the working class would see an influx of energy and dedication. England would begin an era of social reform that it would turn to, once again, after the Second World War.

In the political realm, there was conflict between the Conservative and Liberal parties, but with Prime Minister Lloyd George, a controversial Conservative of the time, the government steered toward providing benefits for its war heroes after the Great War. The rise of the Labour Party, a political party of social democrats and unionists dedicated to standing for the common man and working class, took place during the interwar years. The Labour Party would lead much of the political change in these years, as well as after World War II a few decades later. They assisted in changing policies that benefited workers and restored a national industry of development and manufacturing to England. Again, it was their work that would be built upon in later years, after World War II, during Thatcherism. The Labour Party soon became so influential that, during the interwar years, England's government was termed the Labour government, and all decisions were controlled by the majority party. This led to an increase in funding for low-income housing. The Labour Party also extended conversations with the Soviet Union, being one of the first nations to recognize them as such. This would serve them in the war to come. Where the Labour Party faltered was in 1923 when their anti-communist sentiments got the better of them, and they authorized the search and seizure of the *Workers' Weekly* newspaper office, setting off a negative reaction from both the Liberal and Conservative parties. After being tried, the Labour Party was overthrown by the Conservative Party once more. The two parties would argue throughout the next 10 years, alternating between the controlling party in office until 1931, when England finally settled on having a national government. It's important to note, though, that even today the influence of the Labour Party in England is immense, often controlling many of the political decisions for the country as a whole.

On the international stage, the English were watching Germany rebuild its economy and military presence, and they were concerned that they might be headed toward war. In preparation for such an event, they strengthened their ties with Arab nations, securing their oil reserves and trade routes. In 1919, after World War I, the victorious Allied powers had created the League of Nations. This created a new kind of union among the nations of the new world. It created a series of requirements that all of the nations involved would follow, including a reduced arms presence and open conversation between all nations regarding security and military decisions. In short, the League of Nations supplied accountability to the countries involved after the war, ensuring that no country could go undetected and all were considered represented in the world. As one of the leading countries that were part of the League of Nations, England was committed to its relationship throughout the next several years.

England also underwent social changes in the interwar years. For instance, there was a general decline of religious values and traditions throughout these years. Some historians attribute this to the aftermath of the war. The age-old argument that God cannot be real if there is so much suffering on Earth rose again following the Great War. But more than that, people began viewing the Church and its customs and beliefs as outdated. The Church of England needed a substantial re-evaluation in order to keep up with the modern world, and when they didn't undergo this, Brits reacted. Sunday school attendance dropped, as did missionary work, volunteerism, and overall membership. The decline of boarding schools also contributed to this change in England. Though the tradition of boarding schools would continue to persist for the next several decades, attendance to the specifically religious boarding schools declined, shifting toward nondenominational boarding schools. As a historically religious country, built on the culture of the Church, this was a startling, though no doubt unsurprising, shift in England's culture. The decline in religion also heralded positive changes for women.

Once society was freed from the traditions of the Church and its views on gender, women saw their chance to begin the suffrage movement once more. Women had gained a foothold in the world of work during the Great War, and they saw this as an opportunity to expand upon the image of equality that they had begun to build out of necessity. During the interwar period, women would finally obtain the right to vote, though their wages would no longer be equal to those of men, as they had been during the war. This would prove to be a continuous battle for women in the modern age.

As the 1930s drew to a close, the area of concern at the forefront of England's radar was the triple threat that seemed to be emerging on the international stage: Germany, Japan, and Italy. Though Germany's economy had been crippled from the reparations forced on it after World War I, the nation had returned with a vengeance under the leadership of Adolf Hitler, a war hero from the First World War. Germany had been building its military technology and presence. Furthermore, Italy had been following suit under Benito Mussolini, and Japan, in the Pacific, under the emperor Hirohito, had also built a substantial military presence. It appeared that the 20th century was quickly becoming one defined by dictatorships. England would feel a mounting sense of pressure from all nations as it attempted to discern which nation posed the greatest threat moving into the rest of the 20th century.

The Second World War: 1939–1945

England's Prime Minister Winston Churchill was famous for many things; an articulate and graceful way of speaking was one of them. He would say of World War II, "This is not the end. But it is perhaps the end of the beginning." This was right in many ways, all of which pointed toward how drastically WWII would change not only the nation of England but also the world at large. World War II would span only six years, and yet it was one of the most formative periods of England's history to date. It was a period of unprecedented violence, destruction, and peril for many countries, but particularly so for England. Its people would be tested again, after having survived World War I only to be thrust once more into the grievances of war.

In truth, the English had been preparing for war with Germany prior to the official start of the war. They had been watching Germany progress toward military prowess, as well as its relations with the Soviet Union improve, and preparing themselves for the possibility that the German beast was no longer slumbering. On

September 1, 1939, Germany made its first move in the Second World War, mobilizing its troops and invading Poland. According to the Anglo-Polish military alliance that England had signed with Poland, they were contractually obligated to come to Poland's aid in the event of invasion. Furthermore, England was already concerned about Germany's growing presence in Singapore, a vital territory of England. If the Germans gained too much power, they would encroach on the British presence there, depriving England of vital resources. Joining with France, its longtime ally from the First World War, England declared war on Germany on September 3, beginning the world war. Other countries would soon follow suit, many of whom had originally been colonies of Great Britain. Australia, South Africa, New Zealand, and Canada each declared war on Germany in support of England in the days following England's declaration.

As Germany pushed forward, invading Poland, Denmark, France, Norway, and Belgium (to name a few), it was England's military that stood as the primary force against Germany. England quickly mobilized troops, having learned from its mistakes in the First World War, and instantly reignited its wartime industries. In 1940, Italy merged with Germany in the war, forming the Axis powers. They had a dangerous presence in southern Europe and began to attack Britain from the Mediterranean side. England's allies in New Zealand, South Africa, and Australia provided ships and troops to aid Britain in defending the southern borders and Mediterranean territories. England's history of colonialism and longstanding relationships with other countries were finally coming to benefit them once more. Many people are well aware of the attack that the Japanese launched in December 1941 on the American military base, Pearl Harbor. But what many are unaware of is that the date was also shared by the attack that the Japanese launched on Malaya, a territory that England had occupied for several decades in an attempt to secure control of China. With Japan's attack on British troops in Malaya, England was officially fighting all three Axis powers and at war on three different fronts.

Winston Churchill

Winston Churchill was certainly not the first Churchill to join British politics. A descendant of the First Duke of Marlborough, and his father, a Tory politician, Winston Churchill had practically been born into England's state government. He served in England's House of the Commons as both a Conservative and a Liberal, an unusual change in politics and one that would serve him well later in life when he needed to appeal to both political parties as prime minister. During World War I, he had been integral in guiding the government toward military advancement. It was Churchill who established the Royal Naval Air Service and helped invent the first tank. In the years leading up to the war, Churchill warned his fellow politicians of the rising nationalism in Germany. He warned that it should not be overlooked and that England should be preparing at the very least, if not subduing Germany immediately before it became a problem of international concern. His fellow Parliament members disregarded him, though, choosing to try and keep England off of Hitler's radar as a solution, obviously to no avail and much to Churchill's disdain.

When Churchill became prime minister in 1940, he inherited an office tainted by poor decisions from the previous prime minister, Neville Chamberlain. In early 1938, Chamberlain had given Germany a piece of Czechoslovakia, a strategy that he hoped would calm Germany and render England an ally instead of an enemy to be attacked. If Germany was given territories, then perhaps it would not wage a war to conquer them. When Germany invaded Poland, the people saw that Chamberlain was not a prime minister fit for wartime, and they replaced him with Churchill. Immediately, Churchill showed the British people that this war would be long and grueling and would demand everything of them. In July 1940, Germany began a three-month-long air raid campaign on England, bringing the war back to the home front. As the war waged, Churchill would not only become a highly respected prime minister, but he would also bring a sense of moral direction and comfort to the British people. He was famous for his speeches, both in Parliament and on the radio. Churchill also worked closely with United States President Franklin D. Roosevelt to create a unified front against the Axis powers. Churchill is heralded as being the leader of the Allied victory in World War II, and yet it was only a few months after their victory that he was ousted. Though this is no reflection on Churchill's leadership or dedication to his country, it was instead further confirmation that he was the prime minister for the war, a man cut of the cloth needed to get England through one of its most trying times.

The Home Front

England had been here before. It had learned in World War I that a world war could not simply be fought on the battlefield, in the trenches, or on the fronts. It was fought from home and outward: An epicenter and its rings of impact. If the English were going to make it through the Second World War, they were going to need to do it with the strength and success of their home front first. Without a home, what were their soldiers fighting for? Beginning in 1938, when England saw Germany, Italy, and Japan all seemingly preparing to attack, it began bolstering its home front for the possibility of war.

Food was one of the paramount concerns for England. After having survived several famines surrounding World War I, the country was resolute in its plans to avoid this as it entered the second war. Building even more on what they had done in World War I, propaganda and the media were massive proponents of the home front effort. They kept civilians focused on what was important during these trying times, and they spread information as the government rolled out new initiatives for the war effort. In 1939, Britain launched the "Dig for Victory" campaign that encouraged civilians on the home front to plant "victory gardens." The idea was simple: if everyone on the home front was supplying gardens for themselves and their immediate family, then the agricultural and farming industry could be devoted to supplying food for the troops. Furthermore, it wouldn't place as much stress on those industries as more and more men were called away to serve in the war. In urban areas, victory gardens were even more popular. The government planted these to help bolster city food supplies, taking the pressure off of the ration system, and it helped to build morale among the people. With victory gardens, they had a common goal and a common source of fulfillment. Victory gardens would help to keep the British people fed and their spirits high, even as England instituted rationing, one of the hallmarks of wartime.

Rationing was necessary for several reasons, though it comes with only negative connotations. Images of cookbooks teaching young women how to cook a meal with only water, flour, and a mushroom come to mind, as well as soup lines and ragged faces. Rationing was crucial for England during wartime, and for all countries during the Second World War. Rationing on the home front limited people to the bare essentials in order to reduce waste. It also reduced the need for the import and export industries, freeing up the harbors and ships for military use. England was predominantly an import state: It imported 20 million tons of food each year to feed its ever-growing population. This included fruits, vegetables, cheeses, and grains. Germany knew this and sought to target England's shipping routes for attacks, hoping to starve its citizens. To reduce their shipping needs and combat some of the attacks that did still happen, the Ministry of Food instituted rationing in response to the shortages. Citizens were given an allotment of each type of food that they were allowed to buy on a weekly basis, limiting each household's consumption. In truth, it's difficult to tell how much this aided England, given the rationing horror stories alone, but it's equally difficult to say how many more people would have died from starvation had rationing not been in place. At the heart of the effort was England's dedication to its country at large, proving once again that the British were a benevolent people, willing to stand strong for their country's efforts. This, too, would hold true in the work industries.

England didn't have Rosie, who was the United States' inspiration, but it's quite possible that they didn't really need her. Though England still worked closely with the United States, and Winston Churchill had instituted an agreement with the States to supply them with munitions and other military supplies, England knew that it couldn't accept all of its materials from the United States. Importing everything put England at risk for attacks and being left with nothing with which to face the Germans. England ramped up productions, converting all of their factories into munitions production sites to increase its inventory. The nation began building aircraft, seeing that this was the new way of warfare. They built more tanks and ammunition, attempting to prepare for the unforeseeable future. Though Churchill warned the British people that the war would be long, it would go on even longer than they had anticipated, demanding more of them with each year that passed.

The Theaters

One of the most difficult challenges for England during World War II was juggling all of the different theaters. England was quickly coming to regret their colonial past as they entered the war, with British presence all over the globe. The British Empire had not yet fallen, and England was still very present in multiple territories outside of its own. Unfortunately for them, there was not just one enemy in World War II but four. The Axis powers knew about

England's claims in different areas of the world and divided themselves among England's stakes to weaken it from each side. As a result, there were not simply the Western and Eastern Fronts of the war, as there had been in World War I. World War II elevated what the world knew of warfare in the previous world war, bringing it to an extent no one had seen before. The war became so big that it expanded beyond fronts and, instead, ushered in an age of theaters.

The world broke up into the European Theater, the Pacific Theater, and the Mediterranean and Middle East Theater. Most of England's fighting took place in the Middle East and European Theaters, though in the early days of the war, it also had troops in the Pacific Theater as well. While other countries were typically involved in only one or two theaters, England had stakes in them all from its colonial pasts. The Japanese were the enemy heading the Pacific Theater while Italy headed the Middle East, and Germany headed the European Theater.

To begin, Italy, led by dictator Benito Mussolini, hoped to create the next Roman Empire by conquering the surrounding lands. The Italians attacked Greece and Yugoslavia, countries that England had previously controlled, and were met with British forces, holding them off. But Germany realized that they needed allies, and when Hitler allied with Mussolini, he sent troops to Greece and Yugoslavia, successfully defeating the British. As the war progressed, both German and Italian forces would continue to creep into the Middle Eastern and Northern African countries, where England had maintained sovereign control and regulations over the oil production there. Germany was a militarized state, though, and, heading the Axis powers, declared that the Middle East and Southern Africa were the places that they needed in order to win this world war. The Germans divided their resources among the two theaters, keeping British forces spread thin. For much of the war, the territories would appear to be headed toward German control, though England would keep its forces there for the duration of the war. It wouldn't be until the United States entered the war with fresh reserves and military equipment that the Allied powers would see victory in the Middle Eastern and African theaters.

The Pacific Theater involved the countries of Australia, New Zealand, China, Japan, and the Philippines, along with other islands surrounding the larger countries. It began in 1941 when Japan declared war and invaded

Hong Kong, Borneo, and Malaya. England had holds in all three areas, previously controlling Hong Kong as a withstanding colony inside of China. They had oil reserves in Borneo and Malaya, making Japan's declaration especially threatening. The two countries would wage war for the next four years, eventually resulting in an Allied victory when the United States joined the fight and helped to defeat the Japanese military, which didn't have the same military reserves, and Germany, who proved harder to defeat. Though there would be animosity between England and Japan for the next several decades, in modern England today, Japan is recognized as one of England's closest allies.

The European Theater is by and large the most commonly spoken of and well-known theater in World War II. It saw the creation of concentration camps, housed the Holocaust, witnessed the first use of atomic weapons, and eventually the defeat of the most powerful dictators in history to date. It was within the European Theater that the world saw the Axis powers first break. When the war first broke out, the Axis powers were comprised of the Soviet Union, Italy, and Germany. But Hitler betrayed Stalin, the dictator of the Soviet Union, and launched an invasion of the Soviet Union from the southern side. Stalin then became an Allied power, aiding in the defeat of Hitler by the end of the war. Early in the war, in 1940, Germany overtook both France and Belgium so quickly and with so much force that awaiting British troops retreated to Dunkirk, one of the most famous retreats of the war due to the sheer number of British troops lost in a single battle. With France under Germany's control, the Germans turned their attention to England next. Germany launched a barrage of air raids and attacks in what Winston Churchill would call "The Battle of Britain." Though it depleted British forces and resources, they did not resign England to Germany, proving a vital victory for the Allied powers.

It was at this point that Germany turned on the Soviet Union, seeking to expand its territory east if it couldn't be expanded west. German troops easily breached the Soviet Union's borders, pushing all the way to the major city of Stalingrad. Once there, though, Germany met its match with the overwhelming number of troops on the Soviet side. The Battle of Stalingrad would be one of the bloodiest battles of the entire war, completely wiping out Germany's sixth company. After this battle, Germany would never recover and would spend the remainder of the war slowly being pushed back to Berlin on this front.

In 1941, after Japan bombed Pearl Harbor, the United States entered the war and sent troops to Normandy to liberate France. After discussing strategies with Woodrow Wilson, the president at the time, he and Winston Churchill decided that this would be the most successful course of action. England was still closely allied with France and obligated to protect and defend its neighbor country, but since France had been overthrown by German troops at the start of the war, in order to uphold their relationship, the English needed to regain France. As another major player in the Allied powers, England needed France to regain its strength and home front if they were going to win the war. The Battle of Normandy, also known as "the storming of the beaches," was another turning point for the Allied forces. With British troops storming a cluster of beaches occupied by Nazi soldiers and U.S. troops storming another series of beaches, the two Allied powers soon defeated the Nazi presence on the French coastline and began pushing inward, slowly liberating all of France. The final push in the French region was the Battle of the Bulge in 1944, one of the last battles in the war and the European Theater. Though this was technically an American victory, it allowed British troops to push into Nazi forces from the south and west, leaving only the Eastern Front for the Soviet Union to press into Berlin. Through the collective tactics of the Allied forces, they were able to defeat the Nazi forces in 1945, ending the Nazi regime.

The End of the War

More than 25% of Europe's overall economy had been consumed by the end of the war in 1945 ("United Kingdom home front," 2022). Britain had placed 55% of its labor force into the war effort ("United Kingdom home front," 2022), leaving the country with a stunted economy and workforce, which had likewise shrunk considering the casualties that England suffered in the war. The United Kingdom had lost over 450,000 people in World War II, including those from the crown's colonies who had died fighting. Coming from this set of circumstances and moving forward, England would try to greet its new society in a world that was attempting to repair itself as well. Coming out of World War II, the only country that could be leaned on for financial assistance and that had not been touched culturally and detrimentally on the home front was the United States. They were fortunate, in that the war had never touched their own borders, outside of Hawaii with the bombing of Pearl Harbor. England, as well as the other countries in

Europe, was not so fortunate. England was faced with rebuilding itself once more and, arguably, more comprehensively than it had before in the aftermath of World War I.

Before countries could begin rebuilding themselves on an independent basis, they each knew that there was reconciliation to be done on an international level. England was familiar with the way of the new world, in that it could not practice isolation and think it could remain a strong kingdom. Politics were played through relationships and accountabilities, and the world had failed this responsibility in the buildup to World War II. Nations had ignored warning signs and did not have the political infrastructure in place to act as a single, strong unit, even once they accepted the signs of impending war and potentially dangerous dictatorships. What had previously been known as the League of Nations, the collective agency of protection and alliances among nations after World War I, would evolve into the United Nations after World War II. While the initial plans for the organization were actually formed between Franklin D. Roosevelt, the then-current President of the United States, and Prime Minister Winston Churchill, it was perfected and put into place after World War II.

In the middle of the war, after the United States had entered the conflict, Churchill and Roosevelt both knew that they needed a new organization to help ensure peace across the globe. They knew that something needed to be improved upon so that this wouldn't happen again. Roosevelt had already discussed the idea with Stalin during the war, and with the three largest Allied powers on board with the idea, plans for the United Nations were solidified. In 1944 at the end of the war, China, England, the USSR, and the United States all met to discuss the details of the organization. They wanted something more solid than the League of Nations, and the powers needed to be less abstract in this new collective. At the meeting, they agreed upon four key principles of the United Nations: to obtain and agree upon international peace, to keep the relationships between countries cordial in order to avoid conflict, to achieve cohesive cooperation among nations, and to discuss possibilities and events that would make the previous principles a reality, instead of stagnated ideals. In other words, where the League of Nations had simply stood for international peace, the United Nations would strive for and achieve it, creating a world of prosperity, equality, and justice. As they continued to meet, these principles would only be the first in a series of articles that the UN would uphold. In 1945, the United Nations held its first official meeting, solidifying a new headway into the modern world.

England, following World War II, would undergo many changes. It would continue to strengthen its relationship with the United States. This would only become more fruitful an allyship as England continued into the 20th century with Thatcherism and its mirror image, Reaganism. The end of the war also signaled a change in morality and society. There was no more gray area when it came to personal or national freedoms, and some of England's last colonies would realize this. World War II had been a breach of freedoms in every way. The Holocaust had shown to religious and national cultures that to be discriminated against, in any way, was a violation of one's human rights and that this discrimination could escalate quickly and rampantly. Furthermore, the liberation of the Jewish people, those most affected by the Holocaust, showed people all over the world that a community could come back from persecution, no matter the scale. The modern world would not be one of control but one of independence. England would be most directly affected by this as it sought to repair its economy while steadily losing some of its oldest and most reliable sources of income: Its colonies.

CHAPTER 9

Modern England

While it's true that the world wars were not all that happened in the 20th century, they did impact England for the entirety of it. The previous chapter is not called "The World at War" simply because the entire world fought for 100 years. It is called this because the world faced consequences for the duration of the century for the wars that were fought. Even though both world wars had drawn to a close by the halfway mark of the 20th century, their events would continue to dictate England's actions for the rest of the century, and arguably even beyond. A world war is nothing to scoff at. Two world wars are certainly not to be disregarded for their weight, and England would be bearing this weight for the time to come.

The Decline of the British Empire

Britain's colonies had long been a signal of its wealth and success. They offered England valuable income, materials for exports and imports, and areas of allied support, which had proven especially valuable in the past 50 years. But the world had survived wars and witnessed the consequences of one country controlling the fate of another, and Britain's colonies began seizing their own independence. In 1947, India, previously "the crown jewel" of the empire, would be the first to declare its own independence in the era of what would later be termed England's decolonization. The prime minister of India at the time called on Gandhi, who had advocated for Indians to pull away from Britain back in the 1920s, as inspiration for their resistance. Tensions with Britain rose at the close of WWII, and after the economic strains of the war, England quite frankly didn't have the money to combat India's resistance. Furthermore, Japan was pushing into Southeast Asia, creating yet another risk factor for England to weigh. As a result, England's Prime Minister Clement Attlee resigned control of India that year, granting them their freedom.

Once India broke free of colonialism, other colonial powers saw this as their time to move into the modern age as well. On a social and cultural level, the world was moving away from accepting and embracing the concept of having colonies at all. In 1932, *Time Magazine* had recognized Gandhi as the Man of the Year, creating the lasting image of heroes as those who pushed against colonialism. This shifting mindset of the general public was dangerous for England and meant that its empire could no longer stand as the modern age progressed. The media portrayed Britain negatively as it tried to contain its colonies, placing extra pressure on them to relinquish control. In 1957, Ghana became the first of many African countries to overthrow British rule, declaring themselves a free nation. Seeing this as the end of the British Empire as they knew it, in 1960, Prime Minister Harold Macmillan gave the famous "Wind of Change" speech that expressed to the British public and government at large that decolonization was the way of the new world, and they would have to accept it.

Though England tried to regain some of its colonies in the Soviet Union during the Cold War, a conflict that strained the Soviet Union due to problems with the United States, England failed in this as well. In 1997, when Hong Kong was given back to China, Britain had essentially lost all colonial control short of Australia. By the end of the 20th century, what

England had known as its untouchable empire, the most powerful kingdom that the world had known since the Roman Empire, had disintegrated.

The Welfare State: 1945–1979

After the war, the social issues of England were glaringly apparent. When politician William Beveridge wrote "The Beveridge Report," he identified five "Giant Evils" that England had to tackle coming out of the war. According to the report, if the English were going to recover from the first half of the 20th century, they would have to focus their energy, finances, and politics on five areas of social reform: squalor, ignorance, want, idleness, and disease. England was in need of desperate and comprehensive social reform, and for the next 30 years, its government would institute a litany of acts that completely revitalized England's education, healthcare, and labor systems.

In 1944, England passed the Butler Act, which freed education for all British citizens. This education act abolished fees for secondary school and did away with the age restrictions for sectors within schools that broke up children by age, rather than ability, making the minimum amount of years that a child was required to be in school much longer than before. It also provided school meals and education for adults through community colleges and for younger children through nursery schools. In June 1946, England passed the National Insurance Act, which created the British equivalent of America's Social Security system. It required all working adults to pay a contribution toward receiving sick, unemployment, and retirement benefits as well as other allowances. This act would be improved upon in 1951 when the Butler Act's list of contributions would become more specific and inclusive of those who benefited. In 1966, it would be replaced entirely by the Social Security Act. The criticism that the National Insurance Act received for its disregard for mothers, specifically, was solved with the passing of this next act in August, which provided family allowances for mothers in the UK. The year 1948 saw a slew of social reform bills passed, including the Children's Act, the National Health Service Act, and the National Assistance Act. Through these three new reforms, England readdressed the Poor Laws, which provided welfare for the homeless and had been in effect since Medieval times. They also provided free basic healthcare for British citizens and, under the Children's Act, created a social-care system for orphaned or abused children. By 1979, England's social system was entirely modernized and finally strong enough to support the new modern nation that it had created. Though it appears, on paper, as an overwhelming amount of change in a short amount of time, it would prepare the British citizens for the next 20 years under one of their most influential prime ministers yet.

Thatcherism: 1979–1990

Margaret Thatcher is notorious for a reason, and it is not simply because she was the first female prime minister of Britain. Margaret Thatcher had earned her seat as Prime Minister through an early life in both law and politics. She served as the secretary of state under the returned Conservative government in 1970, earning a reputation as a ruthless and strict conservative. England had nearly bankrupted itself in the previous years with its fervent institution of social reform, and Thatcher would set her sights on repairing this and restoring England's economy once and for all. In 1979 when she was appointed Prime Minister, she brought England into an era of staunch conservative politics, which would later be termed "Thatcherism." In her first term, Thatcher sought to undo some of the social reforms that England had instituted in the previous 30 years. She limited some of the school reforms, including free lunch. She was also faced with a brief war against Argentina, to which she reacted quickly, ending it before her first term was up. Thatcher also turned her attention toward battling the inflation that had risen substantially in the past decades. She limited the funds distributed to housing, healthcare, and other social reform organizations. Though her efforts actually led to rising unemployment, the British citizens saw hope in her strategies to fix England's economy and elected her for a second term.

In Thatcher's second term, her conservatism rang loud and true as she shifted Britain's economy back to a centralized model. She returned industries to England, privatizing state-owned companies that controlled transportation, oil, and other extremely fiscally beneficial industries. She encouraged supply-side economics and a free market, structures that she was sure would reignite the economy. Thatcherism also became defined by the more cultural characteristics of independence and freedom. As Thatcher limited the involvement of the state government, citizens began to see that this was less a political game and more a way of life and cultural shift for England. Though England had started as an independent country, in the past centuries, its government had preached the ideals of collectivism and colonialism. It had formed relationships with other countries and sought to protect the insurance of all its citizens with social reform, but this had cost England its strength as an independent country. It was under Margaret Thatcher that the country tried to regain this strength.

Unfortunately, Thatcher's strategies were fairly unsuccessful. Though her ideals mirrored those of Ronald Reagan in the United States, the two countries' successes were not equal in terms of their economies. Under Thatcher, unemployment did not decrease, and though she reduced funds sent to social reform organizations, she did not decrease government spending substantially. In addition, England's inflation rate was not lower than it was when she took office in 1979. Still, though, she is heralded as a monumental prime minister in England's history for the steps that she took to try and institute change. She has become known as "the Iron Lady" for her fierce determination and her willingness to face every challenge she inherited during her terms.

Brexit

In 1975, the President of the United States, Gerald Ford stated that Europe's economy as well as the Western world at large was stronger for England's involvement in the European Union/United Kingdom conglomerations. In truth, they were a key player in the union, as one of the oldest countries in Europe. Despite challenges over the years, England had the strongest economy and the most established forms of trade, which bolstered everyone's economies. The English were also vital in supporting the development of other countries that later joined the European Union. This was, at its heart, a symbiotic relationship. So then, why, in 2016, would England begin the formal process of leaving the European Union?

Since its inception after World War II, the European Union had been the social and political collection of 27 nations, mostly from the European region. It sought to maintain peace and economic prosperity after the war, collectivizing European nations under one jurisdiction and market. It was supposed to unify the strength of each country's economy as well as strengthen the relationships each country had with one another. As a result, the European Union was, in itself, its own governing body that acted as an umbrella government for all of the countries within the union. If the EU passed legislation, then each country had the option of implementing it. For the most part, many of the countries were content with this system, but as the years went by and England regained its footing after WWII, the English were eager to become completely independent again. Eventually, its relationship with the EU placed more stress on England than it did to ensure its peace and success as a country.

One of the largest contributing factors to England leaving the EU was its policies toward immigration and foreigners. As you well know by now, England had a complicated relationship with immigrants over its centuries of existence. But as England continued through the 20th century, and even moving into the 21st century, the sheer amount of immigrants coming into England would prove a discomfort for many Brits. The EU had a welcoming immigration policy for foreigners from the Middle East and North Africa, but since England had historically established itself as a safe territory for immigrants, it was being flooded with the immigrants coming into Europe and choosing to take refuge in England rather than other EU countries. Some politicians in Britain hoped to amend this and saw that leaving the EU might be a solution.

Economically speaking, England also had issues with how the European Union was handling the financial challenges of the 21st century. With the recession in 2008 and a 20% unemployment rate across southern Europe (Mauldin, 2016), England was displeased with the lack of solutions the EU provided as a collective . Comparing itself to Germany, which enjoyed a 4% unemployment rate at the same time (Mauldin, 2016), England felt itself at a disservice due to its economic responsibilities with the European Union. Many believed that staying in the EU would stagnate their economy, leaving them in a system of the past while other countries were free to move forward.

A second reason for England leaving the EU could be owed to Margaret Thatcher and the rise of nationalism that she encouraged during her terms as prime minister. One of the resounding qualities of Thatcherism was a sense of self-sufficiency and independence, supported by the return of industry to England and the reduced power of the state. It was this nationalism that encouraged some Brits to support Brexit. Though organizations such as the EU, NATO, and the IMF were created with countries' security and insurance in mind, England began to view them as antiquated and only applicable to the problems they had faced immediately after WWII. In the modern world, it behooved England to stay within the contractual obligations of organizations such as the EU, seeing the connection as a restriction rather than a benefit to England as a whole. After 2008, the English felt they had no other choice besides breaking from the EU in order to reclaim their own control of the country.

Thirdly, when it came to voting for Brexit, there were three parties deciding on the end result. Both the Conservative and Liberal parties were in support of remaining within the European Union, but a third party, which had broken from both of them, was for formal separation. The party that broke from the two established parties was one working against the elite. The common people had lost faith in their government, feeling that the politicians who had supported the union from the start had lost their right to control the fate of the country. As a result, when the third party won a majority over the established two, passing the "leave" vote from the EU, it signaled a change yet again in England's history. The people had won, once more, exerting pressure over the English elite and exhibiting the weight that their votes and their representation carried in political policies. Once and for all, England was a country of the people.

CONCLUSION

To say that England's history is rich is to call a perfect gelato delicious. It is an oversight, a gross underappreciation, and an insignificant evaluation. But there is no other way to say it. There is no other way to express the sheer vast nature of England's history in a single sentence. Perhaps it is better to say that England's history is complex, or, perhaps still, that it is as endless as the river Nile. Though, even the river Nile meets an ocean. Even complexity knows its limits. England knows neither end nor true limit.

England has been around for over 800,000 years, a value that is quite nearly unparalleled; what else is this old? What else has withstood as much and continued living, thriving, and growing for this many years? In that time, England has established quite possibly one of the most influential and powerful nations in the world. It began, as any true beginning should, with immigrants, people who were each an unknown to one another. It was born out of warfare, in all truth, and it would wage wars true to its form for many years to come. England created itself, created a system, where there was previously nothing. A group of immigrants and foreigners, people who were not wanted in other regions, came to England and created a kingdom. In all honesty, England created the American dream before there was an America.

England laid the groundwork for political systems that other modern countries sought to recreate and that countries that have yet to establish themselves are still trying to mimic today. England is credited with being the birthplace of some of the most important art of the modern world. Without England, there would be no Shakespeare, who is credited with many of the tropes and ideas of modern literature. Without England, there would not have been Charles Darwin, and without the brave embrace of intellect and logic during England's Age of Enlightenment, the theory of evolution would never have been shared for the world to know.

England is the mother of colonialism, plain and simple. Though it is a marred history and a lineage of corrupt power and overt control over innocent people, it is a crucial part of history and the construction of empires. England's colonies became lasting, independent nations. They became strong and integral parts of the international trade and political spheres. It's possible to claim that without England's influence to begin with, they might not have been introduced as seriously to other countries. This is sad but quite possibly true. England as a country, as a nation, and as a kingdom carries weight. Its name as a nation—and the British people themselves—carries influence.

Without England's influence, Winston Churchill, a man famous for his bravery, his headstrong nature, and his pride for his own country, would never have been able to play such a key role in World War II, the worst war that the world has known to date. England would remain a haven for immigrants, opening its borders to people from all over Europe and, eventually, all over the world. It would redefine what it meant to be a nation, what it meant to be a kingdom. Though it would not be until Benito Mussolini rose to power in Italy in the early 20th century that someone would speak of building the next Roman Empire again, it is safe to say that it was, in fact, England who came the closest to this endeavor.

Today, England is no longer a colonial powerhouse. It is a vital trade partner, an ally to many nations, and the head (even still) of Europe. When one thinks of Europe, one likely still thinks of Rome, but mostly it is England that comes to mind. It takes a truly strong nation to build a kingdom so famous and powerful as the United Kingdom, only to break from it and remain intact. England is solitary now, perhaps more than it has been in centuries. But moving forward, one need only look to the past to predict England's future. The nation will not only survive; it will thrive. It will continue to influence the world. England will continue to lead the world in many spheres, lighting the way for things to come.

Appendix: Kings, Queens, and Prime Ministers of England

What follows in this chapter is less a narrative and more of a reference table. In your continued studies of England's history, it will be difficult to keep all of the monarchs and Parliament heads straight throughout the years. This book is a tool, one that can be used throughout your studies. This chapter is meant to benefit you throughout this book and beyond, as you continue to track England's robust history. You will find that you recognize quite a few of these monarchs and prime ministers from the previous chapters. Many of them had received credit and substantial ink to their names and their reigns throughout history. Others have not garnered such a reputation and will not seem familiar. Let it be known that this is not to indicate the insignificance of some rulers and prime ministers but is, rather, an unfortunate effect of an abbreviated book of English history. Simply put, there isn't enough time and space to discuss every single one of England's monarchs and prime ministers. You, the reader, would be here for the rest of time, and that's only if the book itself was ever finished (a highly unlikely feat in itself). All of the following monarchs and prime ministers have contributed, in some way, to the development of England's history. They are included here to act as a comprehensive list so that you can, perhaps, pursue your own studies on one or several in the future.

Norman Kings
- William I (The Conqueror), 1066–1087
- William II (Rufus), 1087–1100
- Henry I, 1100–1135
- Stephen, 1135–1154

Plantagenet Kings
- Henry II, 1154–1189
- Richard I (The Lionheart), 1189–1199
- John I, 1199–1216
- Henry III, 1216–1272
- Edward I, 1272–1307
- Edward II, 1307–1327 (deposed)
- Edward III, 1327–1377
- Richard II, 1377–1399 (deposed)

The House of Lancaster
- Henry IV, 1399–1413
- Henry V, 1413–1422
- Henry VI, 1422–1461 (deposed)

The House of York
- Edward IV, 1461–1483
- Edward V, 1483–1483
- Richard III, 1483–1485

The Tudors
- Henry VII, 1485–1509

- Henry VIII, 1509–1547
- Edward VI, 1547–1553
- Mary I (Bloody Mary), 1553–1558
- Elizabeth I, 1558–1603

The Stuarts
- James I, 1603–1625
- Charles I, 1625–1649

Lord Protectors
- England became a republic for 11 years from 1649 to 1660, and the Commonwealth of England was declared on May 19, 1649.
- Oliver Cromwell, 1653–1658
- Richard Cromwell, 1658–1659

The Restoration
- Charles II, 1660–1685
- James II, 1685–1688
- William III, 1689–1702
- Mary II, 1689–1694
- Anne, 1702–1714

The Hanoverians
- George I, 1714–1727
- George II, 1727–1760
- George III, 1760–1820
- George IV, 1820–1830
- William IV, 1830–1837
- Victoria, 1837–1901

The House of Saxe-Coburg-Gotha
- Edward VII, 1901–1910

The House of Windsor
- name changed in 1917 due to the anti-German feelings in Britain at the time.
- George V, 1910–1936
- Edward VIII, June 1936–December 1936 (abdicated)
- George VI, 1936–1952
- Elizabeth II, 1952–2022
- Charles III, 2022–Present

Prime Ministers
- Lord John Russell, 1846–1852
- Edward Smith Stanley, 1852–1852
- George Hamilton Gordon, 1852–1855
- Henry John Temple, 1855–1858
- Edward Smith Stanley, 1858–1859
- Henry John Temple, 3rd Viscount Palmerston, 1859–1865
- Lord John Russell, 1865–1866
- Edward Smith Stanley, 1866–1868
- Benjamin Disraeli, the Earl of Beaconsfield, 1868–1868
- William Ewart Gladstone, 1868–1874
- Benjamin Disraeli, 1874–1880
- William Ewart Gladstone, 1880–1885
- Robert Gascoyne-Cecil, 1885–1886
- William Ewart Gladstone, 1886–1886
- Robert Gascoyne-Cecil, 1886–1892
- William Ewart Gladstone, 1892–1894
- Archibald Primrose, 5th Earl of

Rosebery, 1894–1895
- Robert Gascoyne-Cecil, 3rd Marquess of Salisbury, 1895–1902
- Arthur James Balfour, 1902–1905
- Sir Henry Campbell-Bannerman, 1905–1908
- Herbert Henry Asquith, 1908–1916
- David Lloyd George, 1916–1922
- Andrew Bonar Law, 1922–1923
- Stanley Baldwin, 1923–1924
- James Ramsay MacDonald, 1924–1924
- Stanley Baldwin, 1924–1929
- James Ramsay MacDonald, 1929–1935
- Stanley Baldwin, 1935–1937
- Neville Chamberlain, 1937–1940
- Sir Winston Churchill, 1940–1945
- Clement Attlee, 1945–1951
- Sir Winston Churchill, 1951–1955
- Anthony Eden, 1955–1957
- Harold Macmillan, 1957–1963
- Sir Alec Douglas-Home, 1963–1964
- Harold Wilson, 1964–1970
- Edward Heath, 1970–1974
- Harold Wilson, 1974–1976
- James Callaghan, 1976–1979
- Margaret Thatcher, 1979–1990
- Sir John Major, 1990–1997
- Tony Blair May, 1997–2007
- Gordon Brown, 2007–2010

- David Cameron, 2010–2016
- Theresa May, 2016–2019
- Boris Johnson, 2019–2022
- Liz Truss, September 2022–October 2022
- Rishi Sunak, 2022–Present

FREE BONUS FROM HBA: EBOOK BUNDLE

Greetings!

First of all, thank you for reading our books. As fellow passionate readers of History and Mythology, we aim to create the very best books for our readers.

Now, we invite you to join our VIP list. As a welcome gift, we offer the History & Mythology Ebook Bundle below for free. Plus you can be the first to receive new books and exclusives! Remember it's 100% free to join.

Simply scan the QR code to join.

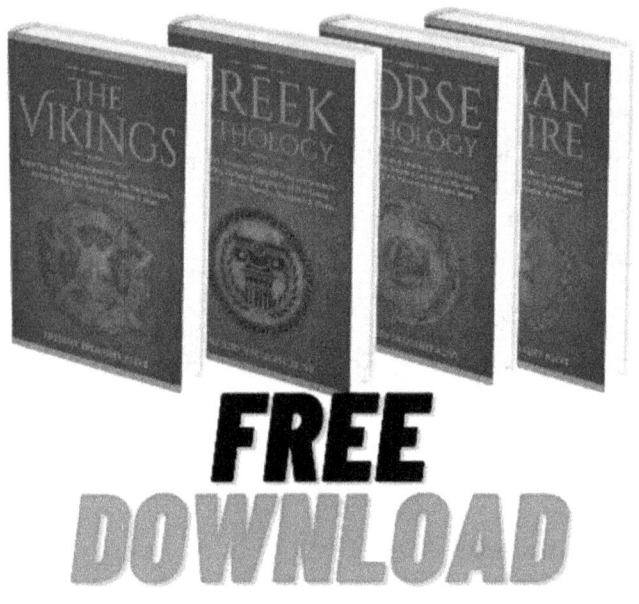

Keep up to date with us on:
YouTube: History Brought Alive
Facebook: History Brought Alive
www.historybroughtalive.com

REFERENCES

The Age of Enlightenment. (n.d.). History Guild. https://historyguild.org/the-age-of-enlightenment/

Anglo-Saxons: A brief history. (n.d.). Historical Association. https://www.history.org.uk/primary/resource/3865/anglo-saxons-a-brief-history

Beck, E. (2022, March 3). *The impacts of the Black Death.* History Crunch. https://www.historycrunch.com/impacts-of-the-black-death.html#/

Beer, G. (2015, November 11). *The impact of On the Origin of Species.* OUPblog. https://blog.oup.com/2015/11/academic-impact-charles-darwin/

Biography.com Editors. (2020, December 2). *Margaret Thatcher.* Biography. https://www.biography.com/political-figure/margaret-thatcher

British Empire. (2022, November 2). In *Wikipedia.* https://en.wikipedia.org/w/index.php?title=British_Empire&oldid=1119562285

British Empire in World War II. (2022, November 3). In *Wikipedia.* https://en.wikipedia.org/w/index.php?title=British_Empire_in_World_War_II&oldid=1119836413

British entry into World War I. (2022, October 26). In *Wikipedia.* https://en.wikipedia.org/w/index.php?title=British_entry_into_World_War_I&oldid=1118331534

Brooke, B. (August 30, 2022). *The legend of King Arthur.* British Heritage. https://britishheritage.com/history/legend-king-arthur

Carlin, D. (2019, September 17). *Roosevelt, Churchill and the creation of the United Nations.* Forbes.

https://www.forbes.com/sites/davidcarlin/2019/09/17/roosevelt-churchill-and-the-creation-of-the-united-nations/?sh=3f1378dc528e

Cartwright, M. (2019, December 18). *Henry III of England*. World History. https://www.worldhistory.org/Henry_III_of_England/

Chan Laddaran, K. (2015, November 11). Poll says Charles Darwin's 'On the Origin of Species ' is the most influential book. CNN. https://www.cnn.com/2015/11/11/world/charles-darwin-irpt/index.html

The Editors of Encyclopedia Britannica. (n.d.). Restoration. In *Encyclopedia Britannica*. https://www.britannica.com/topic/Restoration-English-history-1660

Education Act 1944. (2022, October 31). In *Wikipedia*. https://en.wikipedia.org/w/index.php?title=Education_Act_1944&oldid=1119151657

Elisha Sawe, B. (2019, April 23). *Biggest religions in England*. WorldAtlas. https://www.worldatlas.com/articles/biggest-religions-in-england.html

The end of the British Empire after the Second World War. (n.d.). Imperial War Museums. https://www.iwm.org.uk/history/the-end-of-the-british-empire-after-the-second-world-war

The English Renaissance. (n.d.). Study Smarter. https://www.studysmarter.us/explanations/history/the-tudors/the-english-renaissance/

European Theater of World War II. (n.d.). History Crunch. https://www.historycrunch.com/european-theater-of-world-war-ii.html#/

Fairy tale origins thousands of years old, researchers say. (2016, January 20). BBC. https://www.bbc.com/news/uk-35358487

Frum, D. (2016, June 24). *Why Britain left*. The Atlantic. https://www.theatlantic.com/international/archive/2016/06/brexit-eu/488597/

Harrison, J. (n.d.). *Who were the Anglo-Saxons?* British

Library. https://www.bl.uk/anglo-saxons/articles/who-were-the-anglo-saxons

History.com Editors. (2018, August 21). *Hundred Years' War*. History. https://www.history.com/topics/middle-ages/hundred-years-war

History.com Editors. (2019, June 7). *Winston S. Churchill - Biography, death and speeches*. History. https://www.history.com/topics/british-history/winston-churchill

History.com Editors. (2020a, May 21). *The English Restoration*. History. https://www.history.com/this-day-in-history/the-english-restoration

History.com Editors. (2020b, June 30). *War of the Roses*. History. https://www.history.com/topics/british-history/wars-of-the-roses

History.com Editors. (2021a, September 20). *English civil wars*. History. https://www.history.com/topics/british-history/english-civil-wars

History.com Editors. (2021b, October 21). *Magna Carta*. History. https://www.history.com/topics/british-history/magna-carta

History.com Editors. (2022, September 20). *Revolutionary War*. History. https://www.history.com/topics/american-revolution/american-revolution-history

History.com Staff. (2018, August 29). *Was King Arthur a real person?* History. https://www.history.com/news/was-king-arthur-a-real-person

History of the United Kingdom during the First World War. (2022, October 26). In *Wikipedia*. https://en.wikipedia.org/w/index.php?title=History_of_the_United_Kingdom_during_the_First_World_War&oldid=1118271438

How many Catholics are there in Britain? (2010, September 15). BBC. https://www.bbc.com/news/11297461

Interwar Britain. (2022, September 13). In *Wikipedia*.

https://en.wikipedia.org/w/index.php?title=Interwar_Britain&oldid=1110032981

An introduction to Victorian England. (n.d.). English Heritage. https://www.english-heritage.org.uk/learn/story-of-england/victorian/

Japan-United Kingdom relations. (2022, October 27). In *Wikipedia*. https://en.wikipedia.org/w/index.php?title=Japan%E2%80%93United_Kingdom_relations&oldid=1118523371

Johnson, B. (n.d.). *Robin Hood*. Historic UK. https://www.historic-uk.com/HistoryUK/HistoryofEngland/Robin-Hood/

Kidadl Team. (2022, October 14). *Vikings and Anglo-Saxons facts you should definitely know*. Kidadl. https://kidadl.com/facts/vikings-and-anglo-saxons-facts-you-should-definitely-know#:~:text=Vikings%20and%20Anglo%20Saxons%20were%20t

Knowles, R. (2015, April 21). *The Whigs and the Tories*. Regency History. https://www.regencyhistory.net/2015/04/the-whigs-and-tories.html

Lambert, T. (2021, June 22). *Britain in the 20th century*. Local Histories. https://localhistories.org/britain-in-the-20th-century/#:~:text=Britain%20changed%20hugely%20during%20the%2020th%20century.%20Life,class%20at%20the%20beginning%20of%20the%2020th%20century.

List of prime ministers of the United Kingdom. (2022, November 3). In *Wikipedia*. https://en.wikipedia.org/w/index.php?title=List_of_prime_ministers_of_the_United_Kingdom&oldid=1119823727

Longley, R. (2019, July 28). *Glorious Revolution: Definition, history and significance*. ThoughtCo. https://www.thoughtco.com/glorious-revolution-definition-4692528

Mahabal, P. (n.d.). *Interesting facts about the Tudor and*

Henry VIII Navy. Elizabethan England Life. https://elizabethanenglandlife.com/thetudorsfacts/interesting-facts-about-the-tudor-and-henry-viii-navy.html

Mauldin, J. (2016, July 5). 3 reasons Brits voted for Brexit. Forbes. https://www.forbes.com/sites/johnmauldin/2016/07/05/3-reasons-brits-voted-for-brexit/?sh=756103661f9d

Medieval England history: Life in the Middle Ages. (n.d.). Medieval Ages. https://www.middleages.org.uk/medieval-england/

Mediterranean and Middle East theatre of World War II. (2022, October 23). In *Wikipedia*. https://en.wikipedia.org/w/index.php?title=Mediterranean_and_Middle_East_theatre_of_World_War_II&oldid=1117784696

National Geographic Society. (2022, May 20). Norman Conquest. In *National Geographic*. https://education.nationalgeographic.org/resource/norman-conquest

Nollason, N. (n.d.). *Who were the Dane Vikings?* Vikings Brand. https://www.vikingsbrand.co/blogs/norse-news/danes-vikings

Ohlmeyer, J.H. (2022, September 6). English civil wars. In *Encyclopedia Britannica*. https://www.britannica.com/event/English-Civil-Wars

The Peasants' Revolt. (n.d.). BBC. https://www.bbc.co.uk/bitesize/topics/z93txbk/articles/zyb77yc

Perkins, M. (2019, August 27). *Scotland's Jacobite Rebellion*. ThoughtCo. https://www.thoughtco.com/jacobite-rebellion-4766629

Pierce, D. (2009). Decolonization and the collapse of the British Empire. *Inquiries Journal*, 1(10), 1. http://www.inquiriesjournal.com/articles/5/decolonization-and-the-collapse-of-the-british-empire

Population in the Victorian era. (n.d.). The

Circumlocution Office. https://www.thecircumlocutionoffice.com/times/population/

Population of England 2016. (n.d.). UK Population 2016. https://ukpopulation2016.com/england/#:~:text=POPULATION%20OF%20ENGLAND%20IN%202016%3A%20With%20more%20than,United%20Kingdom%2C%20representing%2084%25%20of%20the%20joined%20total

Pym, H. (2013, April 8). Margaret Thatcher: How the economy changed. BBC. https://www.bbc.com/news/business-22073527

Queen Elizabeth I: Colonising America. (n.d.). Royal Museums Greenwich. https://www.rmg.co.uk/stories/topics/queen-elizabeth-i-colonising-america

Soaft, L. (2022, March 2). *Tudor history: The complete overview.* The Collector. https://www.thecollector.com/tudor-history-overview/

SociologyBri. (n.d.). *The British Welfare State 1945–1979.* Time Toast. https://www.timetoast.com/timelines/the-british-welfare-state-1945-1979

Staff Writer. (2020, March 27). *What were the major turning points of WWI?* Reference. https://www.reference.com/history/were-major-turning-points-wwi-8220d1d85253a1ba

Staff Writer. (2020, April 4). *What were the causes and effects of the Glorious Revolution?* Reference. https://www.reference.com/history/were-cause-effects-glorious-revolution-2c5929b7d08654eb

Steinbach, S. (2022, August 24). Victorian era. In *Encyclopedia Britannica.* https://www.britannica.com/event/Victorian-era

United Kingdom home front during World War II. (2022, September 16). In *Wikipedia.* https://en.wikipedia.org/w/index.php?title=United_Kingdom_home_front_during_World_War_II&oldid=1110641279

Vaijayanti, P.M. (n.d.). *British Empire during Victorian era*. Victorian Era. https://victorian-era.org/british-empire-victorian-era.html

Vaijayanti, P.M. (n.d.). *Victorian era poetry characteristics & salient features*. Victorian Era. https://victorian-era.org/victorian-era-poetry-characteristics.html

Wallenfeldt, J. (n.d.). Acts of Union: Uniting the United Kingdom. In *Encyclopedia Britannica*. https://www.britannica.com/story/acts-of-union-uniting-the-united-kingdom

Wand, H. (2020, April 7). *Jack and the Beanstalk origins*. Fairy Tale Central. https://thefairytalecentral.com/jack-and-the-beanstalk-origins/

White, M. (2018, June 21). *The Enlightenment*. The British Library. https://www.bl.uk/restoration-18th-century-literature/articles/the-enlightenment/

Whitelock, D., & Chaney, W.A. (n.d.). Anglo-Saxon England. In *Encyclopedia Britannica*. https://www.britannica.com/place/United-Kingdom/Anglo-Saxon-England

World War I (1914–1918) - Introduction. (n.d.). History of England. https://www.historyofengland.net/wwone

World War 2 Allies. (2014, August 24). World War 2. https://worldwar2.org.uk/world-war-2-allies

Young, C. (Ed.). (2017, November 21). *England during the war: How the home front did its bit*. England Explore. https://englandexplore.com/england-during-world-war-ii/

OTHER BOOKS BY HISTORY BROUGHT ALIVE

Available now in Ebook, Paperback, Hardcover, and Audiobook in all regions.

The History of England

For Kids:

THE HISTORY OF ENGLAND

We sincerely hope you enjoyed our new book ***"The History of England"***. We would greatly appreciate your feedback with an honest review at the place of purchase.

First and foremost, we are always looking to grow and improve as a team. It is reassuring to hear what works, as well as receive constructive feedback on what should improve. Second, starting out as an unknown author is exceedingly difficult, and Amazon reviews go a long way toward making the journey out of anonymity possible. Please take a few minutes to write an honest review.

Best regards,
History Brought Alive
http://historybroughtalive.com/

www.ingramcontent.com/pod-product-compliance
Lightning Source LLC
Chambersburg PA
CBHW050233120526
44590CB00016B/2071